GUARD YOUR HEART

Purity, Perseverance, His Presence, & the Power of Prayer

GUARD

purity, perseverance,

YOUR

His presence, &

HEART

the power of prayer

AUDREY PHILLIPS JOSE

WhiteFire
PUBLISHING

GUARD YOUR HEART

Copyright © 2014, Audrey Phillips Jose

All rights reserved. Reproduction in part or in whole is strictly forbidden without the express written consent of the publisher.

Unless otherwise noted, scriptures quoted are taken from the Holy Bible, New International Version®, NIV®. Copyright © 1973, 1978, 1984, 2011 by Biblica, Inc.™ Used by permission of Zondervan. All rights reserved worldwide. www.zondervan.com The "NIV" and "New International Version" are trademarks registered in the United States Patent and Trademark Office by Biblica, Inc.™

Scriptures noted NRSV are taken from the New Revised Standard Version Bible, copyright 1989, Division of Christian Education of the National Council of the Churches of Christ in the United States of America. Used by permission. All rights reserved.

Scripture quotations marked NLT are taken from the Holy Bible, New Living Translation, copyright © 1996, 2004, 2007 by Tyndale House Foundation. Used by permission of Tyndale House Publishers, Inc., Carol Stream, Illinois 60188. All rights reserved.

Scriptures noted MSG are taken from *The Message*. Copyright © 1993, 1994, 1995, 1996, 2000, 2001, 2002. Used by permission of NavPress Publishing Group.

Scripture notes GNT are taken from the Good News Translation - Second Edition, Copyright 1992 by American Bible Society. Used by Permission.

Scripture noted NCV are taken from the New Century Version®. Copyright © 2005 by Thomas Nelson, Inc. Used by permission. All rights reserved.

Scripture quotations marked "TLB" or "The Living Bible" are taken from The Living Bible [computer file] / Kenneth N. Taylor.—electronic ed.—Wheaton: Tyndale House, 1997, c1971 by Tyndale House Publishers, Inc. Used by permission. All rights reserved.

WhiteFire Publishing
13607 Bedford Rd NE
Cumberland, MD 21502

ISBNs: 978-1-939023-43-8 (print)
978-1-939023-44-5 (digital)

*To my daughters Christina and Karin,
and to my husband Brian,
my steadfast encourager and biggest fan.*

INTRODUCTION

I came across a photograph one day of a surfer waiting on a wave. In that wave swam a shark. What was running through this surfer's mind? What did he do? What do you do when you're happily riding the surf, and all of a sudden, behind the wave appears what looks to be a shark? Whoa!

In *Guard Your Heart* we are going to look at David, Daniel, Elijah, and Joseph, who each had a "whoa" moment like this—more than one, in fact—and examine how each lived out the principles in Proverbs 4:23-26:

> *Above all else, guard your heart, for it is the wellspring of life. Put away perversity from your mouth; keep corrupt talk far from your lips. Let your eyes look straight ahead, fix your gaze directly before you. Make level paths for your feet and take only ways that are firm.*

David guarded his heart by seeking God's presence everywhere in his life, in all the varied and unexpected circumstances he found himself in.

Daniel "put away perversity from his mouth" by making choices that enabled him to lead a pure life, free of corruption or compromise.

Elijah didn't always look straight ahead, however he persevered in unexpected ways.

Joseph's life underscores the power prayer has to connect us to God, even as his situation went from bad to worse.

These guys were swimming along, enjoying the surf, when behind the wave of promise appeared a shark—a real "whoa" moment—when they had to ask what was going on and why.

I believe it disappoints God when we crystallize the lives of people in the Bible down to one or two highlights (or lowlights) of well-known stories and fail to look more deeply at where this person's story began, how it ended and, more importantly, what we can learn from them.

Old Testament principles lived out in the lives of these people in the Bible reflect God's teaching to the Church of today.

PART 1

PRESENCE

Above all else, guard your heart, for it is the well-spring of life (Proverbs 4:23).

The New Living Translation puts it this way: "Guard your heart above all else, for it determines the course of your life." Your heart is the essence of who you are. In this passage, King Solomon says it is the "wellspring of life"—the source of everything else in a person's life. Thoughts, speech, and actions come from an overflow of the heart. What is in your heart now, is how you are and will be—if the heart is right, so will your actions be. What is in your heart now is how you are and will be—if the heart is right, so will your actions be.

"A good man brings good things out of the good stored up in his heart, and an evil man brings evil things out of the evil stored up in his heart. For the mouth speaks what the heart is full of" (Luke 6:45).

Perhaps Solomon was thinking of his father, David, when he wrote those words in Proverbs, because David was a man who understood this principle and lived it.

David understood that we best guard our heart by welcoming the presence of God into our lives. The world today would have us believe there is no God. There is luck, coincidence, karma—

maybe even a higher power or a "benevolent universe"—but there is no belief in a supernatural presence and intervention in our lives.

God says otherwise:

> *For God, who said, "Let light shine out of darkness," made his light shine in our hearts to give us the light of the knowledge of God's glory displayed in the face of Christ. But we have this treasure in jars of clay to show that this all-surpassing power is from God and not from us* (2 Corinthians 4:6-7).

The treasure Paul is talking about is the presence of Christ in us. Clay jars are fashioned by someone. They can be beautiful, functional, or both. However, clay jars crack; clay jars break. But yet God, in His infinite wisdom, chooses to pour His treasure, His very presence and all which that signifies, into us—people who crack under life's weight; people who are broken.

David Welcomed the Presence of God

David knew the secret of fueling his heart with the presence of God. He became the great leader he was because he intentionally saw God in every area of his life, both good and bad. He recognized God's kindness to him; he acknowledged God's goodness; he experienced His grace. David embraced His mercy and respected His sovereignty. David accepted, and even welcomed, God's personal involvement in his life, even before being anointed as a boy to be Israel's next king (1 Samuel 16:1-13).

When Samuel arrived at David's father's house looking for God's next choice of king, seven brothers were all paraded before him, yet none of these young men were chosen:

> *Samuel saw Eliab and thought, "Surely the*

PART 1: PRESENCE

Lord's anointed stands here before the Lord." But the Lord said to Samuel, "Do not consider his appearance or his height, for I have rejected him. The Lord does not look at the things people look at. People look at the outward appearance, but the Lord looks at the heart" (1 Samuel 16:7).

God was looking for—and found—someone whose heart was drawn to Him. Someone who cultivated a relationship with Him of their own accord.

The presence of God permeated David's life, and it can permeate yours as well, because you are made of the same clay David was. You have the very same treasure in you. You may not know your own potential, but God does. A look at David's life shows how the presence of God impacts a life—molding, shaping, and transforming every decision, every choice, every action, and every attitude.

David's life story has some well-known incidents (killing Goliath with his slingshot and a stone, the seduction of Bathsheba), but there are literally dozens of mini dramas that are recorded about his life. If you feel like you're having a bad day, a bad life, or a "Where is God now?" season, read 1 and 2 Samuel. David had some seriously bad days! And although David led a truly bizarre life, he called it "ordered and secured." At the end of his life he said, "Truly is not my house so with God? For He has made an everlasting covenant with me, ordered in all things, and secured" (2 Samuel 23:5 NASB).

> The presence of God permeated David's life, and it can permeate yours as well, because you are made of the same clay David was.

These are not the words of a man whose God is disconnected with his life. These are the words of a man who was thinking back over his life—as a shepherd, as a member of a king's court, as a fugitive, a warrior, and a king—and saw the presence of God everywhere and at all times. His life is a "How-To Guide" for living in the presence of God.

David Trained Himself to Reflect on God

At the age of about fourteen, David had been anointed to be the next king of Israel, to replace King Saul, yet was then immediately sent back to the sheep, to carry on as before (1 Samuel 16:1-13,18-19). Lest you think this rather picturesque, the life of a shepherd stinks—literally! My husband and I live in Albania, and we come across shepherds from time to time as we're driving to out-of-the-way villages. What always strikes me is their alone-ness. Also the fact that the only thing they carry is their staff. (Where's all their *stuff*? I've never seen a shepherd whip a toiletries bag out of one of their deep pockets!)

During the years he was the anointed king yet wasn't, David could have been impatient and frustrated at the delay, even unsure about his calling, questioning God's direction for his life, making plans for getting out of there—and maybe he was to some extent. Satan utilizes these times to plant seeds of doubt that pollute the wellspring. But what overrode everything, and what guarded his heart, was his confidence that God was in control, and God was not going to leave him in the wilderness forever. To guard your heart, this is an essential first step— having confidence in the truth that your God is in control.

What we see is that David submitted to what was asked of him, and he carried on as before (watching sheep) yet with a sense of deeper purpose. He started writing; training himself to reflect and consider God, himself, where he fit in God's plans for Israel; learning the power of trusting God for his personal safety on a daily basis; and waiting on God's timing for his future. He was searching for God everywhere, writing it down when he found Him, practicing the presence of God in the most humble parts of his boring life with the sheep. (Psalms 8, 18, 19, 23, and 39 are good examples of this.)

Part 1: Presence

Do you have a calling that seems to be at a standstill? Are you barely containing your impatience and frustration, wondering why God isn't moving faster? Or are you taking advantage of the time given you, to learn, grow, gain more experience, and get to know God better, more intimately?

My life in Albania now is very different from the nineteen years I spent in England. There, I was employed, productive, active, involved; here, it's harder because I'm still learning the language, which limits what I can do. Now in my 50s I seem to be starting over, and it's easy to feel like I'm not "doing" anything. But rather than stressing over not being "productive," I am learning to see this season as a time to experience His presence in a deeper way and learning (rather slowly, I admit) to follow David's example of training myself to reflect and consider God and where He's working in my life, learning the power of trusting God, and waiting on God's timing in fulfilling what He's called me to do here.

My challenge is to become a woman who intentionally sees God in every area of my life, unproductive as it may *seem*, to recognize God's kindness and goodness, to practice *seeing* (and acknowledging) His personal involvement in my life. It is not at a standstill by any means from God's perspective.

David Trained Himself to Submit to God

A few years after David was anointed, he was called to King Saul's court, and it was here that God began teaching him how to deal with people, starting with King Saul (1 Samuel 16:14-23). However, as David got more involved in palace life, Saul steadily grew more and more jealous. David experienced God's personal protection as Saul attempted to kill him on three separate occasions. David made a friend, Jonathan, who would have a lasting influence on him. I wonder if he thought, *"Wahoo! This is it, I'm in. Just a matter of time now!"* as he went from accomplishment to accomplishment and his popularity grew:

> *Whatever mission Saul sent him on, David was so successful that Saul gave him a high rank in the army. This pleased all the troops, and Saul's officers as well.... As they danced, they sang: "Saul has slain his thousands, and David his tens of thousands." Saul was very angry; this refrain displeased him greatly. "They have credited David with tens of thousands," he thought, "but me with only thousands. What more can he get but the kingdom?" And from that time on Saul kept a close eye on David.... Saul was afraid of David, because the Lord was with David but had departed from Saul. So he sent David away from him and gave him command over a thousand men, and David led the troops in their campaigns. In everything he did he had great success, because the Lord was with him. When Saul saw how successful he was, he was afraid of him.... When Saul realized that the Lord was with David and that his daughter Michal loved David, Saul became still more afraid of him, and he remained his enemy the rest of his days.... Saul told his son Jonathan and all the attendants to kill David. But Jonathan had taken a great liking to David and warned him, "My father Saul is looking for a chance to kill you. Be on your guard tomorrow morning; go into hiding and stay there"* (1 Samuel 18:5-19:2).

And so things didn't go according to David's plan. He ended up on the run, hiding, and not at all on the course he expected. It would be tempting to see these years of hiding in caves and being constantly on the run as more wasted time. Not just wasted, but downright lonely, desperate, and depressing. Even worse than being a shepherd in the first place!

However, once again we see David submitting, giving up

PART 1: PRESENCE

his need to manipulate events, and in fact, he went a step further: He actively sought the Lord for decisions, deliberately involving God in his everyday life. Time after time we read "David inquired of the Lord" before every move he made, no matter how small it seemed:

- On the run from King Saul and his army, David didn't know where to turn, so he went to the priest, and "Ahimelek *inquired of the Lord* for him" as to where he should go and hide (1 Samuel 22:10, emphasis added).
- Whilst in hiding, the Philistines (Israel's sworn enemy) were looting the farmers' crops. "He *inquired of the Lord*, saying, 'Shall I go and attack these Philistines?' The Lord answered him, 'Go'" (1 Samuel 23:2, emphasis added).
- When his men objected out of fear, "Once again David *inquired of the Lord*, and the Lord answered him" (1 Samuel 23:4, emphasis added). Sometimes one needs confirmation!
- One day David and his men came back from a raid and discovered their camp had been attacked and destroyed by fire, and their wives and children had been taken captive. "David was greatly distressed because the men were talking of stoning him; each one was bitter in spirit because of his sons and daughters. But David found strength in the Lord his God.... And David *inquired of the Lord*, 'Shall I pursue this raiding party? Will I overtake them?' 'Pursue them,' he answered" (1 Samuel 30:6-8, emphasis added).
- Sometimes it got boring, waiting with nothing to do but watch the desert dry. David's army of men would get restless, and it was tempting to do something to alleviate the monotony of the days. It wouldn't be that big a deal to do something to keep the men occupied, but rather than make the decision himself, "In the course of time, David *inquired of the Lord*. 'Shall I go up to one of

the towns of Judah?' he asked. The Lord said, 'Go up.' David asked, 'Where shall I go?' 'To Hebron,' the Lord answered" (2 Samuel 2:1, emphasis added).

- A second time the Philistines came looking for David, who they heard had been anointed king but was in hiding. We're told they came in full force to look for him, and spread out in the valley where he had his stronghold. To me it seems like David could have decided this one himself—the enemy was spread out before him, he was trapped, of course he had to fight. But by now David had learned that no move should be made without drawing God into the decision process. "So David *inquired of the Lord*, 'Shall I go and attack the Philistines? Will you deliver them into my hands?' The Lord answered him, 'Go'" (2 Samuel 5:19, emphasis added). And, in fact, God didn't just tell him to go, He actually spelled out a battle plan for the attack!

- "So David *inquired of the Lord*, and he answered" (2 Samuel 5:23, emphasis added).

And so on. There's a definite pattern here. David was intentionally and consistently bringing God into every decision. He did not go out in his own strength or in his own wisdom. Nothing was too trivial to ask. In doing this, God was able to develop and teach David the next step to spiritual maturity: Seek the Lord in all decisions. This is an essential discipline to develop in the process of guarding your heart. And as it is with any discipline, the more you do it the easier it becomes.

Sometimes, however, we ask for guidance, but when we don't get what we're asking for within the time frame we find acceptable, we take matters into our own hands. Last summer I visited with a friend I hadn't seen in a number of years. As we caught up on our lives, she said this in relation to her being forty-three and still single: "God isn't moving. I've given Him His chance—He's had *years* to give me a husband. If He doesn't care about me, why should I care about Him? I'm going to find someone myself, and if he's not a believer, so what?" My friend was tired of hearing "wait," and she didn't want to hear a "no."

When we genuinely seek the Lord's leading, instead of giving lip service and then proceeding to make our own decisions, we open up channels whereby the Holy Spirit can work; we make ourselves available to Him and allow Him to do what He wants by maintaining a teachable spirit. Because David submitted to God's leading in his life, God was able to teach him the leadership skills he would need as a king: knowledge of men and the power of good governing.

David Trained by God to Deal with People

David's continuing experience of God's protection and deliverance—which built his faith, self-confidence, and diplomatic skills—were lessons he had to learn in order to be an effective leader. It took time. He had a desperate (and rather frightening) group of men to deal with: "All those who were in distress or in debt or discontented gathered around him, and he became their commander. About four hundred men were with him" (1 Samuel 22:2).

As he learned to lead, these men became loyal to David for life. Would a teenager have commanded the same respect of an army if he had been sent straight from shepherd to king? The long and varied discipline of David's early life prepared him for the ultimate task God had planned for him: to be a godly, humble king who would lead God's people in His ways.

Each successive phase of experience developed the conscious dependence on God that was the secret to David's strength throughout his life. Read through the Psalms that David wrote, see how he writes about his experiences, observe how he gives God the glory due Him; use David's method of writing as a pattern for your own endeavors at practicing the presence of God. Notice that he seldom remains focused on himself, and there is a pattern of acknowledging God and His attributes no matter how dire the situation.

When we allow ourselves to be filled with God's presence, it transforms us. In the book of Acts we read of an incident in the lives of Peter and John one day as they were on their way to the temple for prayer. Two ordinary men, doing what they normally did. As they were about to enter the temple, a beggar, unable to walk from birth, asked them for money.

But instead of receiving a few coins, the beggar heard Peter say, "Silver or gold I do not have, but what I do have I give you. In the name of Jesus Christ of Nazareth, walk" (Acts 3:6). Peter took him by the hand, raised him up, and the man entered the temple with Peter and John, walking and leaping and praising God. For the beggar it was a new beginning in his life—for Peter and John it was the beginning of trouble. As a crowd gathered around them, Peter took the opportunity to give the gospel message of Jesus, His death and resurrection, and the need for repentance and forgiveness, which brings new life. And it is while they were speaking that they were arrested by the priests, the Sadducees and temple guards (Acts 4:1-3).

So, Peter—the coward who was always putting his foot in his mouth—and John—who hadn't yet said very much—were brought before the Sanhedrin Council, the equivalent to our Supreme Court, and don't imagine for a minute that Satan wasn't bombarding them with accusations. "Remember that night? You ran away, who do you think you are? You're pathetic!" But the healed man had come with them and was jumping up and down right beside them, giving them a visual reminder of the power they'd just called upon.

The Sadducees, menacing and aggressive, asked them a direct question, "By what power or what name did you do this [healing]?" (Acts 4:7).

Well, that's all Peter needed—they couldn't have asked a better question. And the same Peter who a couple of months before had trembled before a young servant girl and denied Jesus with curses, now spoke with a boldness that proved there is power in the name of Jesus—power to transform an ordinary person into a Spirit-filled hero, because, "When they saw the courage of Peter and John and realized that they were unschooled, ordinary men, they were astonished and they took note that these men had been with Jesus" (Acts 4:13).

This same Jesus is waiting to transform your life, no matter if you feel you're uneducated, untrained, or inadequate for whatever reason. What matters is the time you spend with Jesus. What specific things in your life would show someone today that you "had been with Jesus"? Would people be able to recognize in you the presence of God?

> What specific things in your life would show someone today that you "had been with Jesus"?

During these years as a fugitive, David absorbed and lived with the presence of God. He was not so arrogant as to think that he could control and lead a growing number of hardened men without enablement by a powerful God. It required a teachable spirit on David's part, and was as much a matter of David being faithful to God as it was of God being faithful to David. As his men observed this, it didn't weaken David in their eyes—and I suspect they were watching carefully for *any* sign of weakness—but rather humbly seeking out God's presence *strengthened* his leadership.

David's Crisis of Faith: Where Is God Now?

I imagine you're thinking, "This is all fine, but I'm not King David. He was unique. He knew he was appointed by God—anointed even. He felt God's presence in everything. I don't." Actually, David didn't always *feel* God's presence either.

One time in particular David experienced a serious crisis of faith, when what he said and wrote that he believed about God came up against circumstances in his life that didn't seem to line up with his faith:

> So David and his men, about six hundred in number, left Keilah and kept moving from place to place. When Saul was told that David had escaped from Keilah, he did not go there. David stayed in the wilderness strongholds and in the hills of the Desert of Ziph. Day after day Saul searched for him, but God did not give David into his hands. While David was at Horesh in the Desert of Ziph, he learned that Saul had come out to take his life. And Saul's son Jonathan went to David at Horesh and helped him find strength in God (1 Samuel 23:13-16).

The clay jar that was David was getting a few cracks. This is the Psalm David wrote while hiding in this cave:

> How long, Lord? Will you forget me forever? How long will you hide your face from me? How long must I wrestle with my thoughts and day after day have sorrow in my heart? How long will my enemy triumph over me? Look on me and answer, Lord my God. Give light to my eyes, or I will sleep in death, and my enemy will say, "I have overcome him," and my foes will rejoice when I fall (Psalm 13:1-4).

The cracks of David's crisis of faith were pretty deep here. His beliefs were being called into question. "God said I would be king, but my reality is that I'm filthy, I stink, I'm exhausted, on the run for my life, and *where is God now*?"

Do you wonder if he ever felt betrayed by God? He had put up with *years* of being humble, *years* of being relegated to the background, turning the other cheek, being the better man—and what had it gotten him? What he wrote here indicates that he was pretty close to serious depression, suicidal even: "Give light to my eyes, or I will sleep in death."

Part 1: Presence

Reflecting over your life, looking for God's presence, will bring back memories. Some will be good, some bad. It's not unusual that we mostly remember the things that carry a negative message. "I remember my affliction and my wandering, the bitterness and the gall. I well remember them, and my soul is downcast within me" (Lamentations 3:19-20).

I've often felt like that. Some memories are hard—they're heavy to bear. They keep us captive, replaying the videotape relentlessly over and over in our minds.

In Lamentations chapter three, the first eighteen verses are recalling time after time of hurt, misuse, and abuse, going from bad to worse; but from verse nineteen to the end of the chapter the writer makes a decision:

> *I remember my affliction and my wandering, the bitterness and the gall. I well remember them, and my soul is downcast within me. Yet this I call to mind and therefore I have hope: Because of the Lord's great love we are not consumed, for his compassions never fail. They are new every morning; great is your faithfulness* (Lamentations 3:19-23).

This writer's decision was to call to mind and live in hope because of the Lord's great love and compassion. His decision was to remember the good things God had done for him in the past.

Faith, David's type of faith, is "founded on the memory of God's redemptive acts in the past."[1] The battle for your mind is about what you are going to believe: your own personal litany of hurt, betrayal and confusion; or God's story of His presence with you always.

We cannot help remembering the bad, but we're also to remember and name the moments where God appeared and rescued us. David spent years remembering and recording, which gave him a foundation to build on for the rest of his life. Memory is the key to faith, because remembering what God has done in the past is the basis for our faith in what He can and will do. For instance Rahab, David's great-great-grandmother, when talking to the two men who had come to spy out Jericho said:

> *"I know that the Lord has given you this land and that a great fear of you has fallen on us, so that all who live in this country are melting in fear because of you. We have heard how the Lord dried up the water of the Red Sea for you when you came out of Egypt, and what you did to Sihon and Og, the two kings of the Amorites east of the Jordan, whom you completely destroyed. When we heard of it, our hearts melted in fear and everyone's courage failed because of you, for the Lord your God is God in heaven above and on the earth below. Now then, please swear to me by the Lord that you will show kindness to my family, because I have shown kindness to you. Give me a sure sign that you will spare the lives of my father and mother, my brothers and sisters, and all who belong to them—and that you will save us from death"* (Joshua 2:9-13).

The incidents she was talking about had happened 40 years ago, but her statement of faith in God, "The Lord your God is God in heaven above and on the earth below," was built on what she remembered she had heard about Him, and she knew He was powerful enough to save her in the midst of the destruction that was coming to her people.

David's memories throughout the book of Psalms indicate the depth of his own faith. He didn't just remember God's faithfulness, but he wrote about experiencing God's forgiveness as well. Finding God's presence in your life means in *every* area of your life.

If we were to do a life graph on David it would not look very

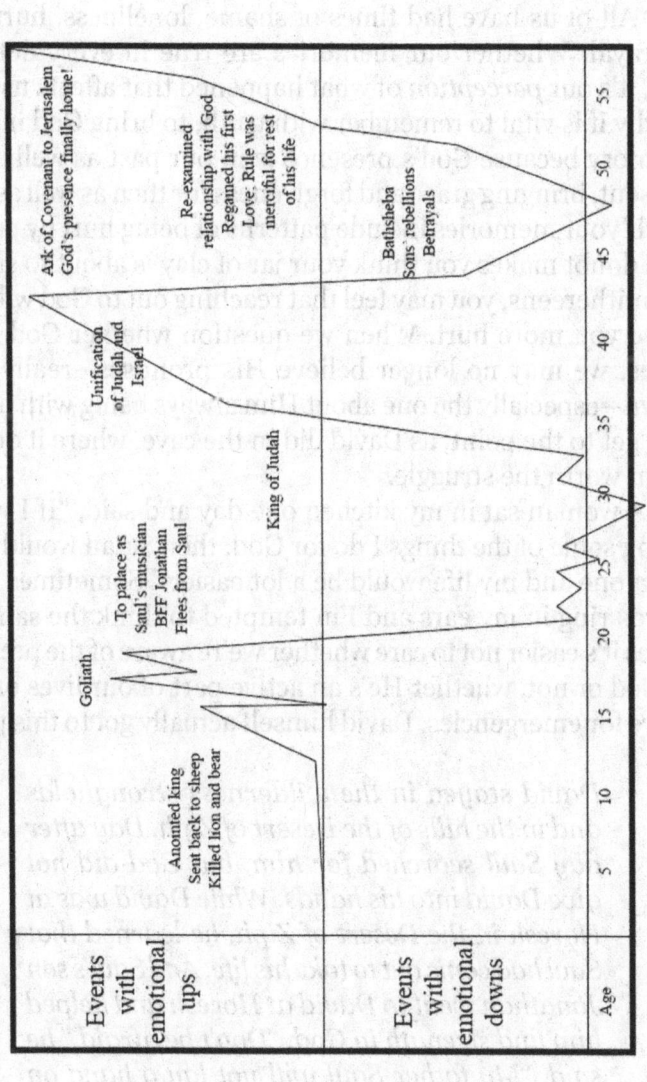

LIFE GRAPH : David - Embraced the Presence of God

inspiring. In fact, his life got so low, it was off the chart.

But David believed otherwise. Remember what he said? "[God] has made an everlasting covenant with me, ordered in all things, and secured" (2 Samuel 23:5 NASB).

All of us have had times of shame, loneliness, hurt, and betrayal. Whether our memories are true in every detail or not, it's our *perception* of what happened that affects us. That is why it is vital to remember with truth, to bring God into the memory because God's presence is in our past as well as our present, bringing grace and forgiveness for then as well as now.

If your memories include patterns of being hurt by people, and doubt makes you think your jar of clay is about to shatter to smithereens, you may feel that reaching out to God will only leave you more hurt. When we question whether God really cares, we may no longer believe His promises—really deep down—especially the one about Him always being with us. We just get to the point, as David did in the cave, where it doesn't seem worth the struggle.

A woman sat in my kitchen one day and said, "If I wasn't doing some of the things I do for God, then Satan would leave me alone and my life would be a lot easier." Sometimes those words ring in my ears and I'm tempted to think the same. At times it's easier not to care whether we're aware of the presence of God or not, whether He's an active part of our lives or only there for emergencies. David himself actually got to this point:

> *David stayed in the wilderness strongholds and in the hills of the Desert of Ziph. Day after day Saul searched for him, but God did not give David into his hands. While David was at Horesh in the Desert of Ziph, he learned that Saul had come out to take his life. And Saul's son Jonathan went to David at Horesh and helped him find strength in God. "Don't be afraid," he said. "My father Saul will not lay a hand on you. You will be king over Israel, and I will be second to you. Even my father Saul knows*

this." *The two of them made a covenant before the Lord. Then Jonathan went home, but David remained at Horesh* (1 Samuel 23:14-18).

In this desolate mountain cave God showed David He was still there by doing two things: First, He made David aware that his life was in danger. Second, miles away, God moved Jonathan to go and seek out his friend David. Sometimes we get so messed up, confused, and overwhelmed, that we need someone to make Him real again. With Jonathan's help, David began to remember what he knew to be true about God, and his faith grew on that.

Encouraging someone in their faith as Jonathan did means to speak the truth to them. But remember (and this can often get lost even with the best of intentions), truth on its own can be harsh. Truth spoken in love changes lives. Not just the truth about the situation but truth about God, because more often than not it's a distorted belief about God that is exacerbating the issue: Is God *really* faithful? Are His promises *really* true? God doesn't offer us a timetable, as David discovered, He offers us His presence. Which was enough for David.

Look at what Jonathan did for his friend: He "helped him find strength in God" (1 Samuel 23:16). This is the best thing you can do for someone who is struggling in their faith and doesn't know where God is, doesn't feel His presence. Not to manipulate the circumstances to make things all better, or try to force God's hand, but rather bring someone back in touch with God and His sovereignty and His plan.

Jonathan did this by listing a string of harsh truths: Yes, my father is looking for you. Yes, he wants to kill you. Yes, you're on the run.

Encouraging someone doesn't mean you try to shield them from reality. Speaking truth is sometimes about showing you understand their difficulties and that you see the situation in the same way they do.

Paul says, "Encourage one another daily...so that none of you may be hardened by sin's deceitfulness" (Hebrews 3:13).

Telling ourselves and each other untruths—to make things easier, to make God easier to understand—isn't helpful, nor is it healthy. And in the long term they won't benefit.

It reminds me of a *Friends* episode where Phoebe decides that a stray cat is her mother incarnate. Her friends try various ways to tell her, without actually coming right out and saying the truth—that what she's got is really just a cat. Finally Ross takes the bull by the horns and says it. Phoebe gets mad because she feels a *real* friend would go along with anything she believes because they are her friend. In other words, a real friend would encourage her to believe anything she wants, wouldn't make her face the reality of truth because it might be something she doesn't want to hear.[2]

That's not a real friend.

Jonathan spoke truth into David's crisis of faith, and David responded—experiencing, as Jesus said, that "The truth will set you free" (John 8:32). When you read this incident, notice that Jonathan doesn't give any advice. He doesn't give a lecture on all things coming together for good. He doesn't try to counsel his friend. What he does is shut up regarding his own opinions, speaks the truth, and points his friend to God.

And this is how David finishes the Psalm he wrote in that cave: "But I trust in your unfailing love; my heart rejoices in your salvation. I will sing the Lord's praise, for he has been good to me" (Psalm 13:5-6). Acknowledging the presence of God in your life is a choice.

David's Training Results: Behavior that Pleases God

For a number of years, King Saul pursued David to the point of being absurd. Chapter 24 of 1 Samuel tells how the king, along with three thousand specially chosen men, chased David from one side of the country to the other. First to Horesh, then to the Desert of Maon, then the Desert of En Gedi, and Saul got closer than he knew in another cave incident. King

Part 1: Presence

Saul actually came into the very cave where David and his men were hiding from him! As Saul was relieving himself, David's men encouraged him to kill the king while he was at his most vulnerable. So David crept forward, unnoticed, and cut off a corner of Saul's robe:

> *Afterward, David was conscience-stricken for having cut off a corner of his robe.* He said to his men, "The Lord forbid that I should do such a thing to my master, the Lord's anointed, or lay my hand on him; for he is the anointed of the Lord." With these words David sharply rebuked his men and did not allow them to attack Saul. And Saul left the cave and went his way (1 Samuel 24:5-7).

This action of not taking things into his own hands, of not killing his enemy, and actually *feeling bad* about what he'd done, was the act of a righteous man. This was a man God had been able to shape as His own, because God was so much a part of who David was.

Look again at David's life graph. Why didn't David kill Saul right then and there and immediately claim his kingship? Because of what he had learned of God over the course of his life about God's personal presence.

God was there when:

- David killed a lion bare-handed.
- he had a face-off with a bear.
- he innocently played his harp for a murderous, jealous king.
- he hunted with Jonathan.
- he slipped from cave to cave for safety.
- He sent Jonathan to David to point him back to Himself.

And God was there with David in that cave as he faced the temptation to murder.

What Happens when You Don't Guard Your Heart?

David had faith; he trusted God, there is no disputing that. However, we can get to a place where we're complacent and let our guard down. When this happens, Satan is right there, ready and waiting, with the temptation to make choices from our own perspective or desires.

What happened when David got complacent, let down his guard, and ignored God's presence in his life? The infamous Bathsheba incident. He committed adultery with the wife of one of his officers, Uriah. And when it became obvious that she was pregnant, David schemed to find some way to hide his sin. First he tried to manipulate circumstances so that Uriah would think the child was his. David sent a message to the commander of the army, Joab, to send Uriah before the king. King David pretended to be interested in news from the battle and then sent Uriah home to his wife...but Uriah refused to sleep in his own house. "Uriah said to David, 'The ark and Israel and Judah are staying in tents, and my commander Joab and my lord's men are camped in the open country. How could I go to my house to eat and drink and make love to my wife? As surely as you live, I will not do such a thing!'" (2 Samuel 11:11).

Next David got Uriah drunk and sent him home...but still Uriah refused to sleep in his home while the armies of Israel were in the field. Finally, David sent Uriah back to the battlefront with a message for Joab which read: "Put Uriah out in front where the fighting is fiercest. Then withdraw from him so he will be struck down and die" (2 Samuel 11:15).

His plan worked—Uriah died on the field of battle. David was free to take Bathsheba as his wife and his sin was hidden. Or so he thought.

Isaiah 29:15 declares: "Woe to those who go to great depths

Part 1: Presence

to hide their plans from the Lord, who do their work in darkness and think, 'Who sees us? Who will know?'"

Hebrews 4:13 tells us: "Nothing in all creation is hidden from God's sight. Everything is uncovered and laid bare before the eyes of him to whom we must give account."

You can't hide anything from God. David thought his sin was hidden. That he'd covered it up. He thought no one would know. But God knew.

It is also important to remember that when you don't guard your heart, it has an impact on others—the repercussions of our choices do not affect just ourselves.

> *Then the Lord sent Nathan to David. And he came to him and said, "There were two men in one city, the one rich and the other poor. The rich man had a great many flocks and herds. But the poor man had nothing except one little ewe lamb which he bought and nourished; and it grew up together with him and his children. It would eat of his bread and drink of his cup and lie in his bosom, and was like a daughter to him. Now a traveler came to the rich man, and he was unwilling to take from his own flock or his own herd, to prepare for the wayfarer who had come to him; rather he took the poor man's ewe lamb and prepared it for the man who had come to him." Then David's anger burned greatly against the man, and he said to Nathan, "As the Lord lives, surely the man who has done this deserves to die. He must make restitution for the lamb fourfold, because he did this thing and had no compassion." Nathan then said to David, "You are the man! Thus says the Lord God of Israel, 'It is I who anointed you king over Israel and it is I who delivered you from the hand of Saul. I also gave you your master's house and your master's*

wives into your care, and I gave you the house of Israel and Judah; and if that had been too little, I would have added to you many more things like these! Why have you despised the word of the Lord by doing evil in His sight? You have struck down Uriah the Hittite with the sword, have taken his wife to be your wife, and have killed him with the sword of the sons of Ammon. Now therefore, the sword shall never depart from your house, because you have despised Me and have taken the wife of Uriah the Hittite to be your wife.' Thus says the Lord, 'Behold, I will raise up evil against you from your own household; I will even take your wives before your eyes and give them to your companion, and he will lie with your wives in broad daylight. Indeed you did it secretly, but I will do this thing before all Israel, and under the sun'" (2 Samuel 12:1-12 NASB).

David now did a rather unexpected thing—he repented. Often when confronted with our sin, our first instinct is to blame shift, lie, or deny. David did none of those things. He made no excuses, nor did he blame Bathsheba. This man, whom God said was "a man after His own heart" (Acts 13:22), did not disappoint God in how he responded to conviction of his sin. His consistent habit of involving God in every aspect of his life and his close walk with God were not in vain, because David saw God as God, and sin as sin: "Then David said to Nathan, 'I have sinned against the Lord'" (2 Samuel 12:13).

It is when we are truly honest with God that we find His mercy and grace: "Nathan replied, 'The Lord has taken away your sin. You are not going to die'" (2 Samuel 12:13).

"This was an important defining moment in David's life. He confessed his sin, and was prepared to accept his punishment of death. Instead, God showed His grace by forgiving David, and allowing him to live. For the rest of his days, when David

PART 1: PRESENCE

opened his eyes in the morning, he knew that he was alive for one reason and one reason only: the sheer grace of God. That turning point changed the direction of David's life, and deepened his relationship with God to a level he had never known before. Understanding God's grace will have the same effect on you and me."[3]

You cannot hide your heart from God. Psalm 51 is David's prayer of repentance. It shows that it was not just a "sorry, I'll try to do better" sort of thing, but a deep, heartfelt plea to *God* for forgiveness, healing and restoration:

> *Have mercy on me, O God,*
>   *according to your unfailing love;*
> *according to your great compassion*
>   *blot out my transgressions.*
> *Wash away all my iniquity*
>   *and cleanse me from my sin.*
>
> [3] *For I know my transgressions,*
>   *and my sin is always before me.*
> [4] *Against you, you only, have I sinned*
>   *and done what is evil in your sight;*
> *so you are right in your verdict*
>   *and justified when you judge.*
> [5] *Surely I was sinful at birth,*
>   *sinful from the time my mother conceived me.*
> [6] *Yet you desired faithfulness even in the womb;*
>   *you taught me wisdom in that secret place.*
>
> [7] *Cleanse me with hyssop, and I will be clean;*
>   *wash me, and I will be whiter than snow.*
> [8] *Let me hear joy and gladness;*
>   *let the bones you have crushed rejoice.*
> [9] *Hide your face from my sins*
>   *and blot out all my iniquity.*
>
> [10] *Create in me a pure heart, O God,*

and renew a steadfast spirit within me.
¹¹ Do not cast me from your presence
or take your Holy Spirit from me.
¹² Restore to me the joy of your salvation
and grant me a willing spirit, to sustain me.

¹³ Then I will teach transgressors your ways,
so that sinners will turn back to you.
¹⁴ Deliver me from the guilt of bloodshed, O God,
you who are God my Savior,
and my tongue will sing of your righteousness.
¹⁵ Open my lips, Lord,
and my mouth will declare your praise.
¹⁶ You do not delight in sacrifice, or I would bring it;
you do not take pleasure in burnt offerings.
¹⁷ My sacrifice, O God, is a broken spirit;
a broken and contrite heart
you, God, will not despise.

¹⁸ May it please you to prosper Zion,
to build up the walls of Jerusalem.
¹⁹ Then you will delight in the sacrifices of the righteous,
in burnt offerings offered whole;
then bulls will be offered on your altar.

Old Testament law required the hyssop plant for two rituals of purification. Someone healed of leprosy and anyone who had contact with a dead body must be cleansed with hyssop. David knew his sin was a fatal disease that could only be cured by God. Only the grace of God can purify us and forgive our sins.

Genuine repentance brings forgiveness, restoration, and healing, and David committed himself to serving God with his restored life.

In the same way He provided His presence for David, broken and cracked jar that he was, God has provided His presence for us. It doesn't matter how great our sins may be. It doesn't matter how despised we are, how worthless we feel, or how many times Satan accuses us of failing. God loves us as much as He loved David. His presence is there in our lives, even when we don't realize or acknowledge it. We can look at our life graphs and focus on our past, our sins and failures, on the low points, wondering, "Where was God? How could He let this happen? Why did I make that awful choice? How can God use me now? I'm just a broken and glued together clay pot that isn't worth anything!"

Or we can believe God when He says we have His treasure in us, He is with us always, and nothing can separate us from Him. We can make the choice the writer of Lamentations did, to call to mind the good we know to be true about God, and to choose to put our hope in Him.

> Faith is believing that God really has put His Treasure (Jesus) in you.

Use your past to see where God was shaping you, not how He should condemn you. Faith is using your past to strengthen your belief. Faith is believing that God *really has* put His Treasure (Jesus) in you.

Where have you seen God's presence in your life? If you can't see it, ask Him to show you. God is so involved in your life that not only do you have face-to-face intimacy with Him through His Son, but God pours His precious Treasure into a cracked, dull pot. He pours the light of life into you. He pours the knowledge of His glory into you. He pours Himself into you, and with that, the power to withstand opposition, confusion, persecution, and attack.

Because we have Christ in us we're not crushed, in despair, abandoned, or destroyed (2 Corinthians 4:9). We need to guard His presence within us as a treasure, because it's the wellspring of life—for you and for others. It is the source of transforming power, it's a light to the world, and it brings forgiveness and grace.

Do the life graph at the end of this section and see God's hand building your character for a purpose. Resist "seeing" a series of disconnected incidents in your life. Ask Jesus to do it with you—ask Him to show you the *truth* about your memories. Don't see just the clay pot, but see the clay pot with God's Treasure in it. Keep the presence of God in your heart because it is the wellspring of a transformed life. Transformation cannot be accomplished in our own strength; rather it is God's grace and forgiveness that transforms lives.

David began as a boy whose innocence responded to God. He included God as he lived his life, seeking Him out always. He became "a man after God's own heart" (1 Samuel 13:14).

A man after God's own heart—God Himself called David that. Wouldn't we like this to be said about us? If so, we must do as David did:

- He acknowledged God's blessing in the good.
- He acknowledged God's goodness and sovereignty in the bad.
- When confronted with his sin he not only confessed, he repented and didn't repeat the sin.

When we walk with God as David walked with God, we can say with complete confidence that "[God] has made an everlasting covenant with me, ordered in all things, and secured"
(2 Samuel 23:5 NASB).

PART 1: PRESENCE

Practicing the Presence of God in Your Life

1. **Read Psalm 16.**
   Underline, circle, or mark the text that speaks to you.

   Keep me safe, my God,
     for in you I take refuge.

   ² I say to the Lord, "You are my Lord;
     apart from you I have no good thing."
   ³ I say of the holy people who are in the land,
     "They are the noble ones in whom is all my delight."
   ⁴ Those who run after other gods will suffer more and more.
     I will not pour out libations of blood to such gods
     or take up their names on my lips.

   ⁵ Lord, you alone are my portion and my cup;
     you make my lot secure.
   ⁶ The boundary lines have fallen for me in pleasant places;
     surely I have a delightful inheritance.
   ⁷ I will praise the Lord, who counsels me;
     even at night my heart instructs me.
   ⁸ I keep my eyes always on the Lord.
     With him at my right hand, I will not be shaken.

   ⁹ Therefore my heart is glad and my tongue rejoices;
     my body also will rest secure,
   ¹⁰ because you will not abandon me to the realm of the dead,
     nor will you let your faithful one see decay.
   ¹¹ You make known to me the path of life;
     you will fill me with joy in your presence,
     with eternal pleasures at your right hand.

2. What does it say?
Make a verse-by-verse list of the most outstanding, obvious facts. Do not paraphrase—just use words in the text.

3. What does it mean?
What spiritual lessons or principles can be learned from these facts?

4. Now, what does it mean in my life?
Rewrite the lessons/principles from Step 3 in the form of a personal question.

LIFE GRAPH

Events with emotional ups											
Events with emotional downs											
Age	5	10	15	20	25	30	35	40	45	50	55

PART 2

PURITY

Put away perversity from your mouth; keep corrupt talk far from your lips (Proverbs 4:24).

There is something beautiful about the purity of a pearl. Pearls are a product of pain. Somehow the shell of an oyster gets pierced and an abrasive grain of sand gets inside, and it hurts the tender flesh so much that all the healing resources of the oyster rush to that spot, enveloping it in healing fluids that soothe and repair. When the wound is healed a pearl has formed—a tiny, perfect little jewel born of adversity and conceived in stress. Had there been no wound, no pain, no interruption to that oyster's life, there would be no pearl.

Daniel is one such person with the purity of a pearl. Into his life came a painful interruption, the "abrasive grain of sand"—captivity in a foreign land. As we look at the life of this extraordinary man, don't believe for one minute that he didn't experience pain, loss, grief, prejudice, or rejection. Don't think he led a charmed life and things were easy for him. His whole life was a product of the pain of his past.

Living a Pure Life in an Impure World

Before we look at how Daniel lived a pure life in the surroundings of Babylon, we need to begin with a bit of history, because if you're unaware of the background, the significance of biblical narratives loses some of its impact.

The city of Babylon, a great city on the Euphrates River, dominated the ancient world and is first mentioned in Genesis when the city's founder, Nimrod, began building a tower which became known as the Tower of Babel. However, this tower was not built for the worship and praise of God, but rather the builders said:

> *"Come, let us build ourselves a city, with a tower that reaches to the heavens, so that we may make a name for ourselves; otherwise we will be scattered over the face of the whole earth." But the Lord came down to see the city and the tower the people were building. The Lord said, "If as one people speaking the same language they have begun to do this, then nothing they plan to do will be impossible for them. Come, let us go down and confuse their language so they will not understand each other." So the Lord scattered them from there over all the earth, and they stopped building the city. That is why it was called Babel—because there the Lord confused the language of the whole world. From there the Lord scattered them over the face of the whole earth* (Genesis 11:4-9).

The city of Babylon became a source of idolatry for all of the ancient world.[4] In Scripture Babylon is an image of godlessness and an enemy of God's people, Israel; for us today Babylon represents the godless world in which we live. Babylon was where Daniel, along with other royal captives, would soon be living.

The second bit of history we need to look at is the capture and enslavement of the tribe of Judah, which was Daniel's tribe, and also the geographical area of the Southern Kingdom of Judah where his tribe lived. Previously, the nation of Israel had been divided into two kingdoms: Northern and Southern. The Northern Kingdom of Israel fell to the Assyrians in 721 BC, and a little over a century later the Southern Kingdom of Judah fell to the Babylonians.

There were two sins that caused the tribe of Judah to be carried away into captivity, and which seem to be the same two sins believers today are especially prone to struggle with. The first was disobedience to the word of God. The second was a departure from the worship of God, which was something the Israelites had struggled with since leaving Egypt. Since Babylon was the center of idol worship in the ancient world, when God allowed Judah to be taken as slaves to Babylon, He was sending them to the capital city of idolatry.

In effect He was saying, "Since you won't let me cure you of your addiction to idols, I will send you to where they had their origin, back to the source, and there you can learn what idolatry is like. For seventy years you can experience those idols you so desperately want to serve." In fact, after their years of captivity in Babylon, they no longer had a desire to worship idols. God put them in the land of Babylon to learn to hate the false gods they had once worshipped.[5] Our idols of today may not be so blatant, but they lead to destruction just as the people of Judah's habit of turning to idols destroyed them. We must be careful what we attach ourselves to—God may just let us have our fill of it!

This is where we pick up Daniel's story—at the beginning of the Jewish exile as a consequence of centuries of disobedience and false worship.

Obtaining a Pure Life Takes Resolve

When Daniel was taken captive, he was stripped of everything, from his family to his friends and possessions. When he arrived in Babylon he was then stripped of the very last thing that belonged to him: his name.

Then the king [Nebuchadnezzar of Babylon]

> *ordered Ashpenaz, chief of his court officials, to bring into the king's service some of the Israelites from the royal family and the nobility—young men without any physical defect, handsome, showing aptitude for every kind of learning, well informed, quick to understand, and qualified to serve in the king's palace. He was to teach them the language and literature of the Babylonians. The king assigned them a daily amount of food and wine from the king's table. They were to be trained for three years, and after that they were to enter the king's service. Among those who were chosen were some from Judah: Daniel, Hananiah, Mishael and Azariah. The chief official gave them new names: to Daniel, the name Belteshazzar; to Hananiah, Shadrach; to Mishael, Meshach; and to Azariah, Abednego* (Daniel 1:3-7).

The name Daniel means "God is my judge." The new name he was given was "Belteshazzar"; "Bel" being the name of the Babylonian god whom the Canaanites called Baal, who long rivaled Jehovah in the affections of the Hebrew people.[6] Giving the captives Babylonian names was a strategy to remove from them any reference to their God; anything that reminded them of their faith. It was Satan mocking the God Daniel had always worshipped, and the purpose was to subtly suppress his faith. It led to immediate pressure on Daniel.

My name means "noble strength," but people don't go around calling me Noble Strength, they call me Audrey—and in consequence something is lost. In Albania you hear names that are the actual meanings used in conversation; for example, I know Butterfly (Flutura), Rainbow (Ulber), Dove (Pëlumb), Life (Jeta), Good Faith (Besmirë) and Good Luck (Fatmirë). When I use their names I am reminded exactly of what they mean.

Names define us, and they can hold a lot of power, too.

PART 2: PURITY

However, not all the names we give ourselves, or that others give us, are edifying. Remember the childhood taunt, "Sticks and stones can break my bones but names will never hurt me"? That's simply not true. Names can cause us to believe lies about ourselves.

Joe Namath, a football player from the 1970s, once joked that he thought his name was "Shut up" until he was thirteen.[7] It's painful to have a name like that. Maybe you have a name someone else has put on you. Maybe it's one you've put on yourself. The name I gave myself was "unwanted." Was it true? No. But it was a lie I told myself—and believed—for forty-two years. If you believe a lie it will affect how you live, how you treat and respond to others, and not only what you believe about yourself but what you believe about God.

What is the name Satan wants to give you? Failure? Too Late? Ugly? Can't? Barren? Sick? Unwanted? Hopeless? Depressed? Jesus wants you to know your real name: Loved One. Redeemed. Christ's Friend. Joy. Beautiful. I Can. Hope. Rejoiced Over. Wanted. This is one way Satan—the world—tries to exert its power on us. In fact, our true names are so precious that they are given to us by God Himself (Isaiah 62:2).

Daniel refused to believe the lie of the name Belteshazzar. From the beginning he made a stand, not a belligerent or aggressive one, but an assertive stand nonetheless. He would retain his God-given name in his heart, a name that would keep his God always in front of him as a daily reminder of the truth of who he was and Who he served.

Daniel's name, "God is my judge," guided his actions from adolescence through old age. Committed to pleasing God alone, he was unshakeable in his determination to do what he knew was right, determined to live up to his name. This particular group of Jewish captives which Daniel was part of would be exposed to academic and religious ideas of a godless civilization, but he and his three friends made a resolution to remain pure in God's eyes:

But Daniel resolved not to defile himself with

> *the royal food and wine, and he asked the chief official for permission not to defile himself this way. Now God had caused the official to show favor and compassion to Daniel, but the official told Daniel, "I am afraid of my lord the king, who has assigned your food and drink. Why should he see you looking worse than the other young men your age? The king would then have my head because of you." Daniel then said to the guard whom the chief official had appointed over Daniel, Hananiah, Mishael and Azariah, "Please test your servants for ten days: Give us nothing but vegetables to eat and water to drink. Then compare our appearance with that of the young men who eat the royal food, and treat your servants in accordance with what you see"* (Daniel 1:8-13, emphasis added).

I love that word *resolved*. It's so much more than just deciding, it implies an unyielding determination. Why was eating the king's food such a big deal? It was not unlawful in itself for them to eat the king's meat or to drink his wine. However, they felt they needed to be scrupulous concerning the meat, according to the guidelines God set for the nation of Israel to distinguish them as His, separate and holy:

> *"I am the Lord, who brought you up out of Egypt to be your God; therefore be holy, because I am holy. These are the regulations concerning animals, birds, every living thing that moves about in the water and every creature that moves along the ground"* (Leviticus 11:45-46).

Sometimes the meat that would be set before them was expressly forbidden by their law, such as pork; or possibly they were afraid that the food could have been previously offered in sacrifice to an idol, or blessed in the name of an idol.

Daniel, Hananiah, Mishael, and Azariah, were firm in their commitment to stand before their Lord with no shame because of choices they made.

Life is a series of decisions and resolutions. We live on the basis of decisions we make, dozens of them every day—what we intend to do, what we're going to say to people, how we're going to respond to things. What you are today is the result of decisions you've made in the past. What you will be tomorrow is determined by the decisions you make and the stands you take today. Do we really even consider God's will in our daily decisions? David, in Part 1, considered God in everything. Acknowledging God's presence is foundational to developing habits and a lifestyle that choose God's standards of purity over our own watered-down ones.

> What you will be tomorrow is determined by the decisions you make and the stands you take today.

Retaining a Pure Life by Standing on God's Promises

Daniel was at a crisis time in his life. He was about to make a decision which would have repercussions that would affect him his whole life. Again as we saw with David, into every person's life comes a crisis of faith—that little grain of sand invading your smooth oyster shell of a life. You can go for years coasting on the good teaching you've had and times of spiritual growth, but at some point all this is going to be put to the test. You're going to face a time when you have to decide if you really believe God is who He says He is (holy) and does what He says He will do (keep His promises). Daniel would have been brought up on Scriptures such as:

- "God is not human, that he should lie, not a human being, that he should change his mind. Does he speak and then not act? Does he promise and not fulfill?" (Numbers 23:19).
- "You know with all your heart and soul that not one of all the good promises the Lord your God gave you has failed. Every promise has been fulfilled; not one has failed" (Joshua 23:14).
- "Be strong and courageous. Do not be afraid or terrified because of them, for the Lord your God goes with you; he will never leave you nor forsake you" (Deuteronomy 31:6).

Daniel chose to retain and live out his belief in what he had learned growing up in a Hebrew home about the One True God. He could make this resolve in confidence because God was personal to him, not just a concept, something he was taught, or a distant and terrifying God; and Daniel was able to stand on the promises of his God, saying, "Okay, You've commanded us to stay pure, You have always said You would help in time of need, now I'm standing on that promise." Promises that we, too, can claim.

The Apostle Paul says, "Since we have these promises, dear friends, let us purify ourselves from everything that contaminates body and spirit, perfecting holiness out of reverence for God" (2 Corinthians 7:1). Paul himself had many occasions when he was faced with choices, and he was open and honest about his struggles. No matter what was thrown at him, he never turned away from following the truth of God's Word, or from the way his Father led him. Paul followed Christ's example, who also never turned away from following the truth of God's Word, or from the way the Father led Him.

Paul goes on to say that:

Therefore, in order to keep me from becoming conceited, I was given a thorn in my flesh, a

> *messenger of Satan, to torment me. Three times I pleaded with the Lord to take it away from me. But he said to me, "My grace is sufficient for you, for my power is made perfect in weakness." Therefore I will boast all the more gladly about my weaknesses, so that Christ's power may rest on me. That is why, for Christ's sake, I delight in weaknesses, in insults, in hardships, in persecutions, in difficulties. For when I am weak, then I am strong* (2 Corinthians 12:7-10).

There are thorns in everyone's life. Daniel's thorn was his whole life of exile. You probably don't have to think very hard to know what yours is—physical, moral, sexual, educational, emotional, or psychological. Maybe your thorn is an illness. Maybe it's a person. You may even have more than one thorn in the form of challenges you face. Although we don't know what Paul's thorn was, being human, Paul wanted rid of it. He pleaded with God to remove it. It reminds me of Jesus in the Garden of Gethsemane pleading with His Father to remove His thorn—a crown of thorns in fact. Both Jesus and Paul prayed three times and did not receive the answer they prayed for. However, both received answers that were sufficient for their needs. For Jesus, an angel came and ministered to Him. For Paul, God Himself spoke clearly to him: "My grace is sufficient for you." God gave Paul what he needed, His grace, not the thorn-free life Paul wanted. "My strength is made perfect in weakness." It's in times of weakness and hardship that the Lord's strength—power—can be experienced most completely.

Passages like these invite us to ask two questions: What is true power? What is the relationship between power and weakness? God's wisdom gives answers to both these questions that are totally different from the world's wisdom. He wants to pour His power into our lives so our transformed character draws others to Him and inspires Christians to live for Him.

In his book *Enjoying Intimacy with God*, Oswald Sanders speaks of four "thorns" that we can experience:

Disturbance—Because of our inclination to let comfort and good fortune make us spiritually complacent, God allows our lives to be disturbed so that we are cast back on to dependence upon him.... Do you confess this tendency to God and ask him to disturb your life to prevent this? When disturbances come, do you see this good that God wants to bring?

Darkness—God allows us to go through periods of spiritual depression, when the sunshine of his love is obscured by dark clouds. One of the most powerful servants of God, Martin Luther, went through periods of intense spiritual darkness his entire Christian life. God permits this in order to deepen our trust (and ultimately our intimacy) with him.

Disappointment—God is committed to his will and our best interests for our lives. This is why his thwarting of our self-centered plans...is an act of love. But in his wisdom he sometimes even disappoints our plans to serve him...because he knows we are not yet ready, or because he has a better role....

Inequality—God allows us to experience difficulties that others...do not have to go through.... He sometimes delivers others from difficulties that he does not deliver us from. Why did God heal others through Paul, but refuse to heal Paul of his "thorn"? Why did God release Peter from prison, but leave Paul in prison for over 4 years? Depending on our response, these inequalities may precipitate resentment toward God—or they may drive us to cast ourselves more deeply on his loving wisdom so that we often see later the wisdom of God's treatment.[8]

Part 2: Purity

Thorns are a bit like the oyster shell being pierced and the abrasive grain of sand that painfully seeps through. How are you reacting to the "thorns" God is currently allowing in your life? Are you bitter because of them, compromising your values or principles to try and remove the thorns? Or do you trust God and the pearl He is forming in you? He will work through your thorns to reveal your weakness and make you more dependent on Him. If you let Him. This acknowledgment guides you toward greater spiritual power and harvests gratitude for God's wisdom which is sometimes beyond our realm of understanding.

Many things changed in Daniel's life when he was taken into exile—every one of them out of his control. His whole life had become a thorn: He was in another country; removed from all that was familiar; facing new situations; new people who didn't think or believe as he did. Does this ever sound familiar for my own life! Daniel was faced with a choice, as we often are, to either live in obedience to what God had told him to do, or justify it away. Compromise was, and always is, a convenient and sometimes attractive option. Had Daniel compromised his personal beliefs and integrity, no one would have blamed him for doing so:

- The other captives would not have judged him because they faced the same dilemma.
- His parents weren't around to be disappointed in him.
- He could have justified it by telling himself that it's just a little food, it really doesn't matter; after all, one has to eat!
- He could have been goaded by his peers: *"Good grief, don't be so legalistic; it's not strictly what God said, but it will give us an opportunity to witness. How can we win these people if we offend them? What's being asked is perfectly reasonable."*

In what areas of your life are you facing a crisis of faith?

Where are you facing a choice—to obey or justify yourself? It can be the smallest of things. Practical or spiritual. For me it comes down to two words: food allergy. For years I tried to minimize my allergy to gluten, ignore it, tell myself if I didn't read the label I couldn't be held responsible. Then one time I was really ill after deliberately choosing to eat something I knew had gluten in it. It was a "Lord, just take me now" moment, when a voice filled the room and said, "Audrey, stop abusing your body." This may seem like a small thing, but when it's something God speaks to you about, it is not to be ignored or disobeyed.

Many of the choices we make are disobedient ones because we do not realize the significance of the small. God does. The spirit world does. Daniel did. We may think it's not a big deal to be consistent with what we know God has been saying to us, because it doesn't seem all that important in the greater scheme of things. Denial can make disobedience appear less serious, but it's always serious to God.

Daniel was in a place of weakness and hardship, where his faith was tested and challenged every day. It was here where he learned to rely on God's presence, which resulted in an unshakable faith.

A Life of Purity Requires Faith in a Faithful God

Faith means that whether I am physically delivered or not, I will stick to my belief that God is love, God is good, God is truth. Paul lived with the thorn that God did not take away. Daniel's thorns, both physical and emotional, were also not removed: He lived with the loss of home, parents, brothers and sisters, friends, position, security—absolutely everything. Sometimes faith comes down to asking ourselves a few simple questions: Do we believe God is good? Faithful? Just? As we saw previously, David's secret to guarding his heart was a constant awareness of the presence of God. Paul and Daniel's secret was a constant awareness of the faithfulness of God.

In Exodus 34:6, a book Daniel would have known well, God tells us He is good, abounding in love, and He is faithful. The Bible puts the truth that God is faithful with the fact that God cannot change: "I the Lord do not change" (Malachi 3:6).

In fact, God's very name is Faithful: "I saw heaven standing open and there before me was a white horse, whose rider is called Faithful and True" (Revelation 19:11).

This is Someone who will never let you down, who will never break His promise to you. God will be—*must* be—faithful to His Word and to every promise He has made to you in it. *Faithful* means to be absolutely firm in keeping to promises and commitments to another. What are some of the promises of God? The following are just a few verses in which God says He will be faithful to you:

- Through God's faithfulness I am called into fellowship with Jesus (1 Corinthians 1:9).
- He will not allow me to be tempted beyond what I can endure (1 Corinthians 10:13).
- He will strengthen and protect me from the evil one (2 Thessalonians 3:3).
- He can never be unfaithful to me (2 Timothy 2:13).
- He promises to forgive my sins and cleanse me (1 John 1:9).

Jeremiah wrote the book of Lamentations (which means *grieving*) because he was grieving over the destruction of Jerusalem and its people and their spiritual numbness.

He was also going through a particularly nasty time himself, and was at the point of despair. He was threatened (Jeremiah 11); beaten and put in stocks (Jeremiah 20); put in prison (Jeremiah 37); thrown into a cistern full of mud and left to die (Jeremiah 38); forced to go against his will to Egypt all the while prophesying to the king that God had said not to (Jeremiah 43).

This guy was in a pretty low frame of mind. The beginning of Lamentations is a follow-up to the book of Jeremiah, a going over and over of the awful things that had been happening to Jeremiah and the Jewish people. For two and a half chapters, he wallows in self-pity, poor me, poor us...but in the middle of the book, Chapter 3, there's a change:

> Yet this I call to mind and therefore I have hope: Because of the Lord's great love we are not consumed, for his compassions never fail. They are new every morning; great is your faithfulness. I say to myself, "The Lord is my portion; therefore I will wait for him" (Lamentations 3:21-24).

Can you imagine Jesus focusing on these verses when He was standing before Herod, bleeding and in pain? *"But this I call to mind, and therefore I have hope, the Lord is my portion says my soul, therefore I will hope in Him, great is your faithfulness."* Someone spit at Him, others mocked and laughed at Him. *"But this I call to mind, and therefore I have hope, the Lord is my portion says my soul, therefore I will hope in Him, great is your faithfulness."* Someone punched His face. *"But this I call to mind, and therefore I have hope, the Lord is my portion says my soul, therefore I will hope in Him, GREAT IS YOUR FAITHFULNESS!"*

God is, at this very moment, being absolutely faithful to you.

Nowhere in the Bible are we promised that as believers we will not be hurt, or experience ugly, sinful things. God's promises are for enabling us to *overcome* in the face of evil. These are the very promises Jesus hung on to during that dreadful day. *Great is your faithfulness.* God is, at this very moment, being absolutely faithful to you, for He can do nothing else.

Jeremiah deliberately "calls to mind" certain things about God that cannot ever change. He succeeds in getting what he knows about God from his heart to his head. It's a choice, it's what we call faith—giving mental assent to God's faithfulness. *"Yet this I call to mind."* What did Jeremiah call to mind? Three things:

- Loving-kindness that never ceases.
- Compassion that never fails.
- God's faithfulness.

Why would the statement "Great is your faithfulness" be particularly significant for Jeremiah to remember at this time? Because it looked exactly like God *was not* being faithful. Jeremiah had just spent twenty verses dwelling on his affliction, things that had happened to him, and he was feeling pretty bitter. Do you ever do this? Do you dwell on past mistakes? What you don't have? People who insulted you? Your difficult situation? I admit I've answered yes to all these questions at different times in my life. As soon as my head hit the pillow that relentless video would start.

And what is the result? Depression, doubting God, unrest, emotional turmoil. So what are we going to do? Memorize Lamentations 3:21-24 for a start! When everything around us seems to go against God's faithfulness to His promises, when we're in the midst of a crisis of faith, He says, "Trust Me anyway!"

Let Him show His faithfulness to you. (If you haven't done the life graph at the end of Part 1, take time and do it now.)

However, there are a few reasons why we might not be aware of God's faithfulness to us:

- We choose not to see it.
- We focus on the negative side of the situation.
- We're too busy looking toward and worrying about the

future.
- We don't rely on what we know about God.
- We don't know God's Word well enough to stand firmly on His faithfulness.

Daniel, in the testing of faith over eating the king's food, knew and chose to obey the Word of God over the pressure to conform. In this he stood with three others, but there were many more who had been taken captive. These peers of his would most likely be going to other places after three years of training at the king's court (Daniel 1:5). They would be out of his life, but God wouldn't be going anywhere, therefore God's opinion of him was more important to Daniel than what his peers thought of him.

This conscious, deliberate choice of Daniel's to retain his purity was the foundation of his reputation for the rest of his life. He didn't wait until after the allotted three years to make it. He didn't go along with everyone else for three years, then when the test came stand there and say, "Okay, God, it's Your responsibility to get me through this, do Your stuff." Daniel did well not only because God was with him, but because for those three years he had been faithful in keeping his mind and body clean, keeping himself pure, in order to honor and obey God and become a pearl of great price.

Maintaining a Pure Life Requires Obedience

You may be wondering why I keep bringing up obedience with the topic of purity. It's because purity comes out of obedience in all aspects of our lives. We can't wake up one day and decide, "Right. Today I'm going to be pure" and then carry on doing things in secret. For example, Berlin in the 1980s had a blatantly sinful counter-culture. A young man my husband and I knew moved there to plant a church but got caught up in an immoral lifestyle. Why was it so easy for him to be side-tracked? Because two years prior, when he first arrived in Berlin, he had

PART 2: PURITY

made a choice, justifying it as "just fitting in with the culture," to frequent places where he would face constant temptation. Then months later, when it came to a choice to be pure, he couldn't do it. He compromised, and he sank. Not Daniel—he never compromised, and he never sank.

And for Daniel all is well for the next five or six decades... until King Darius:

> *It pleased Darius to appoint 120 satraps to rule throughout the kingdom, with three administrators over them, one of whom was Daniel. The satraps were made accountable to them so that the king might not suffer loss. Now Daniel so distinguished himself among the administrators and the satraps by his exceptional qualities that the king planned to set him over the whole kingdom. At this, the administrators and the satraps tried to find grounds for charges against Daniel in his conduct of government affairs, but they were unable to do so. They could find no corruption in him, because he was trustworthy and neither corrupt nor negligent. Finally these men said, "We will never find any basis for charges against this man Daniel unless it has something to do with the law of his God"* (Daniel 6:1-5 emphasis added).

Daniel was known for an unshakeably pure and incorruptible life, which he could live because of his faith. His faith took root and grew because he guarded his heart. He guarded his heart by living a pure life, first as a young man by not giving in to peer pressure, and then as a leader by resisting corruption. Don't despair if you feel you don't have the faith you need—God is the author of our faith, and in Acts we're told that "He purified their hearts by faith" (Acts 15:9).

God will never require you to do something without

providing the means for you to do it.

> So these administrators and satraps went as a group to the king and said: "May King Darius live forever! The royal administrators, prefects, satraps, advisers and governors have all agreed that the king should issue an edict and enforce the decree that anyone who prays to any god or human being during the next thirty days, except to you, Your Majesty, shall be thrown into the lions' den. Now, Your Majesty, issue the decree and put it in writing so that it cannot be altered—in accordance with the law of the Medes and Persians, which cannot be repealed." So King Darius put the decree in writing (Daniel 6:6-9).

Daniel's reputation remains firm under relentless attack. The decree designed to bring him down began, "Anyone who prays..." What a testimony! The only thing they could find wrong with this guy was that he prayed! The only way to get at him was to insist he go thirty days without praying in public—he could still have prayed with the curtains closed. What would you have done? Honestly? After all, a month isn't so long. I imagine some of us have gone longer without praying. I also imagine Satan tried tempting Daniel with the same old justifications:

- The other captives would not judge him—remember, they were in the same boat.
- His parents weren't there to be disappointed in him.
- He could have justified himself—closing the window would be less offensive.
- His peers would be admonishing him, *"Good grief, don't be so legalistic; it's not strictly what God wants, and it's just a little thing. It really doesn't matter. You can do it in secret."*

Part 2: Purity

> *Now when Daniel learned that the decree had been published, he went home to his upstairs room where the windows opened toward Jerusalem. Three times a day he got down on his knees and prayed, giving thanks to his God,* just as he had done before. *Then these men went as a group and found Daniel praying and asking God for help* (Daniel 6:10-11 emphasis added).

This wasn't a case of "I'll show them!" and throwing open his windows in defiance, or with a belligerent, aggressive attitude. Nor was it a case of Daniel suddenly deciding to get his prayer life in order because things were getting a bit tough. It was as if this decree had never been announced, and Daniel continued to pray three times a day in front of his window, refusing to do anything in secret, unashamed to acknowledge his relationship with God. No one would have blamed him if he'd said, "I don't have to pray out loud, God can hear me anyway. I don't have to go in front of the window, it will just provoke the situation."

Instead, he took a risk on God and...he was thrown to a pack of lions. David, as we saw in Part 1, took risks on God and at times struggled with feeling betrayed; did these thoughts go through Daniel's mind as well?

However (and with God there's always a however!), in the morning when the king ran to the pit he found Daniel alive and untouched. There was no betrayal on God's part—even if at first there appeared to be. Rather, God provided an opportunity to show His strength in Daniel's weakness. Daniel was able to say, "My God [my judge] sent his angel, and he shut the mouths of the lions. They have not hurt me, because I was found innocent in his sight" (Daniel 6:22).

Neither Daniel nor David knew what the outcome would be from taking a risk on God. They only knew they were willing to risk everything for a God they knew to be faithful, whether it seemed as if He was being faithful in that instance or not.

A Pure Life Is Possible for Us

Daniel took a stand against the gods of his time. We can bow to the gods of our time by our desire to pursue status, success, beauty, reputation, or notoriety. We can compromise in our thought life. We can compromise in how we speak, not being quite honest. In what area of your life are you compromising? Maybe it's what you're reading, watching on TV, or how you're spending your time. Have you taken on a bit too much of "the culture," like our friend in Berlin, knowing it goes against God's expressed word? Knowing God has told you something but doing what you want anyway?

Someone once said to me, "I know what God wants me to do, but I don't want to do it—so I'm not going to. Then in a couple of months I'll confess it, and He'll have to forgive me because He promised to." Not only is this compromising, but it's actually mocking God in a spirit of rebellion. We all do it at some time, maybe not as blatantly as this person did, but the attitude is in our hearts all the same.

We'll never again be a teenager, the age Daniel was when he faced his first crisis of faith and made one of the choices that determined the course of his life. We've already made choices, good and bad, and are living with the consequences. But we do have all the same options Daniel had, and it's never too late to put them into play. He had a spiritual reservoir that he drew from when crisis came—and he had more than one in the course of his life in Babylon. Every day he meditated on the truths of God and talked with Him.

When he was taken prisoner I sincerely doubt he was allowed to run back and get a copy of his Scriptures. What would you have if your Bible were to be taken away? My husband once spoke with a Russian pastor who had been a religious prisoner for years, with only one page of the Bible; that one page kept him going. What would you do if your one page was taken away?

When I was young we used to sing a song in church: "Dare

Part 2: Purity

to be a Daniel, dare to stand alone"—make a stand now to see what one person can do when they stand against the tide of conformity.

After hearing me speak on this at a conference, Cindy, a woman in my study group, declared, "I want to be contagious. There are women I want to influence to get into God's Word, but I'm afraid they will judge me, reject me, or be offended." So together she and I committed to pray for these women. First one woman with a desire to make a stand to grow in holiness in her church even though she was afraid of rejection and being misunderstood. Then a handful of women praying. Seven months later, fifty-four women responded by attending an evangelistic outreach Cindy organized with the full support of the very women she had been afraid of.

What Cindy learned was that she *wasn't* alone. It was a lie Satan was using to keep her frozen in an unproductive state. The truth is we are never alone, and not only is the presence of God with us, He has many others in the wings who we aren't even aware of. Making a stand will draw them out.

Let's declare that we're not going to live out of the lies the enemy has given us. Let's declare that we're going to live out of the words that say "I am with you." Words that say, "Nothing can separate you from Me." Words that say, "The same power that was in Jesus is in you." Take a risk on God, live a pure life as He requires, dare to be a Daniel, and see what God will do. Daniel's steadfast witness brought a powerful king to the point of acknowledging God's almighty power. God not only worked a physical miracle, but a spiritual one in the heart of this king:

> *Then King Darius wrote to all the nations and peoples of every language in all the earth: "May you prosper greatly! I issue a decree that in every part of my kingdom people must fear and reverence the God of Daniel. For he is the living God and he endures forever; his kingdom will not be destroyed, his dominion will never end. He rescues and he saves; he performs signs*

and wonders in the heavens and on the earth. He has rescued Daniel from the power of the lions" (Daniel 6:25-27).

Ripped from his home and family, Daniel knew sadness and grief. He began life in Babylon as a teenager who made a stand to keep himself pure and incorruptible. He ended a man with unshakeable determination, untainted, unimpeachable, and unashamed of his God. Leaving as his legacy the refusal to conform to this world and turning a nation—Babylon, the symbol of man's self-sufficiency—to worship the One True God.

A Pure Life

1. **Read Psalm 15.**
   Underline, circle, or mark the text that speaks to you.

   Lord, who may dwell in your sacred tent?
     Who may live on your holy mountain?

   ² The one whose walk is blameless,
     who does what is righteous,
     who speaks the truth from their heart;
   ³ whose tongue utters no slander,
     who does no wrong to a neighbor,
     and casts no slur on others;
   ⁴ who despises a vile person
     but honors those who fear the Lord;
   who keeps an oath even when it hurts,
     and does not change their mind;
   ⁵ who lends money to the poor without interest;
     who does not accept a bribe against the innocent.

   Whoever does these things
     will never be shaken.

2. **What does it say?**
Make a verse-by-verse list of the most outstanding, obvious facts. Do not paraphrase—just use words in the text.

3. What does it mean?
What spiritual lessons or principles can be learned from these facts?

4. Now, what does it mean in my life?
Rewrite the lessons/principles from Step 3 in the form of a personal question.

PART 3

PERSEVERANCE

Let your eyes look straight ahead, fix your gaze directly before you (Proverbs 4:25).

From the diary of John Wesley:

Sunday, A.M., May 5
Preached in St. Anne's. Was asked not to come back anymore.

Sunday, P.M., May 5
Preached in St. John's. Deacons said "Get out and stay out."

Sunday, A.M., May 12
Preached in St. Jude's. Can't go back there, either.

Sunday, A.M., May 19
Preached in St. Somebody Else's. Deacons called special meeting and said I couldn't return.

Sunday, P.M., May 19
Preached on street. Kicked off street.

Sunday, A.M., May 26
Preached in meadow. Chased out of meadow as

bull was turned loose during service.

Sunday, A.M., June 2
Preached out at the edge of town. Kicked off the highway.

Sunday, P.M., June 2
Afternoon, preached in a pasture. Ten thousand people came out to hear me.[9]

Perseverance. It's a powerful, positive force. Like John Wesley, the Prophet Elijah was successful at persevering; his life was one of dogged perseverance. We can relate to him because he struggled with disappointment, disillusionment, and, eventually, spiritual disengagement. This is when we give up because we can't see God's hand anywhere anymore, and we decide that persevering is just not worth it.

Elijah was an important Israelite prophet whose name in Hebrew means "my Lord is Jehovah." Accounts of his life and actions are recorded in the Old Testament books of 1 and 2 Kings. He is regarded as a "reformer" prophet—his purpose was to call the Israelites back to the worship of Yahweh and away from the evil pagan religious cults and Baal worship that were growing in popularity.

Elijah Persevered in God's Strength

Throughout the reigns of the various kings of Israel it was repeatedly recorded that, "they did evil in the sight of the Lord," each one getting progressively worse. But Ahab outdid them all:

> *Ahab son of Omri did more evil in the eyes of the Lord than any of those before him. He not only considered it trivial to commit the sins of Jeroboam son of Nebat, but he also married Jezebel daughter of Ethbaal king of*

PART 3: PERSEVERANCE

> *the Sidonians, and began to serve Baal and worship him. He set up an altar for Baal in the temple of Baal that he built in Samaria. Ahab also made an Asherah pole and did more to arouse the anger of the Lord, the God of Israel, than did all the kings of Israel before him* (1 Kings 16:30-33).

Elijah had been sent repeatedly by God to King Ahab, who was the current king of Israel. This is the first glimpse of Elijah as a person who persevered, because during this period of intense struggle between the kingdom of God (represented by Elijah) and the kingdom of Satan (represented by King Ahab and his wife Jezebel), Elijah marched fearlessly into the palace and confronted Ahab and Jezebel every time God told him to. In fact he did it so often that once when he went before the king with yet another word from God, Ahab said to him, "So, is it really you, you troublemaker of Israel?" (1 Kings 18:17 NLT). He had quite a reputation of persistence!

In 1 Kings 17:1-6 Elijah told Ahab that because of his wickedness in leading Israel away from worshipping the One True God, God was going to hold back the rain for three years. Immediately after Elijah delivered this message, God sent him to a secluded valley where He provided for him during these three years by sending ravens to bring him bread and meat (1 Kings 17:2-6). When God told Elijah to leave the valley, he was penniless and homeless but God still provided for him:

> *Then the word of the Lord came to him: "Go at once to Zarephath in the region of Sidon and stay there. I have directed a widow there to supply you with food." So he went to Zarephath. When he came to the town gate, a widow was there gathering sticks. He called to her and asked, "Would you bring me a little water in a jar so I may have a drink?" As she*

was going to get it, he called, "And bring me, please, a piece of bread." "As surely as the Lord your God lives," she replied, "I don't have any bread—only a handful of flour in a jar and a little olive oil in a jug. I am gathering a few sticks to take home and make a meal for myself and my son, that we may eat it—and die." Elijah said to her, "Don't be afraid. Go home and do as you have said. But first make a small loaf of bread for me from what you have and bring it to me, and then make something for yourself and your son. For this is what the Lord, the God of Israel, says: 'The jar of flour will not be used up and the jug of oil will not run dry until the day the Lord sends rain on the land.'" She went away and did as Elijah had told her. So there was food every day for Elijah and for the woman and her family. For the jar of flour was not used up and the jug of oil did not run dry, in keeping with the word of the Lord spoken by Elijah (1 Kings 17:8-16).

Elijah had learned to trust God so much that not only was he confident God would provide for this woman's immediate needs, but a short time later he raised this same woman's son from the dead (1 Kings 17:17-24). This is a prophet with an impressive track record in taking a fearless stand for God because he knew and had experienced that God *is* who He says He is, and *does* what He says He will do. Elijah had seen God's miraculous intervention, protection, and provision in his own life as well as the lives of others, and he persevered in trusting God for his own safety and needs. Guarding your heart means perseverance becomes an integral part of how you live, a concept well documented throughout the New Testament:

- "Therefore, since we have been justified through

faith, we have peace with God through our Lord Jesus Christ, through whom we have gained access by faith into this grace in which we now stand. And we boast in the hope of the glory of God. Not only so, but we also glory in our sufferings, because we know that suffering produces perseverance; perseverance, character; and character, hope" (Romans 5:1-4).

- "May the Lord direct your hearts into God's love and Christ's perseverance" (2 Thessalonians 3:5).
- "Therefore, since we are surrounded by such a great cloud of witnesses, let us throw off everything that hinders and the sin that so easily entangles. And let us run with perseverance the race marked out for us" (Hebrews 12:1).
- "Consider it pure joy, my brothers and sisters, whenever you face trials of many kinds, because you know that the testing of your faith produces perseverance. Let perseverance finish its work so that you may be mature and complete, not lacking anything. If any of you lacks wisdom, you should ask God, who gives generously to all without finding fault, and it will be given to you" (James 1:2-5).
- "For this very reason, make every effort to add to your faith goodness; and to goodness, knowledge; and to knowledge, self-control; and to self-control, perseverance; and to perseverance, godliness; and to godliness, mutual affection; and to mutual affection, love. For if you possess these qualities in increasing measure, they will keep you from being ineffective and unproductive in your knowledge of our Lord Jesus Christ" (2 Peter 1:5-8).
- "To the angel of the church in Ephesus write: These are the words of him who holds the seven stars in his right hand and walks among the seven golden lampstands. I know your deeds, your hard work and your perseverance" (Revelation 2:1-2).

The next major incident recorded in Elijah's life is a confrontation on Mount Carmel, where God and His prophet Elijah faced off against King Ahab, but this time the stakes were higher: "Then Elijah stood in front of them and said, 'How much longer will you waver, hobbling between two opinions? If the Lord is God, follow him! But if Baal is God, then follow him!' But the people were completely silent" (1 Kings 18:21 NLT). First Kings 18 recounts this dramatic encounter and the triumph of God's power:

> *Later on, in the third year of the drought, the Lord said to Elijah, "Go and present yourself to King Ahab. Tell him that I will soon send rain!" So Elijah went to appear before Ahab.... When Ahab saw him, he exclaimed, "So, is it really you, you troublemaker of Israel?" "I have made no trouble for Israel," Elijah replied. "You and your family are the troublemakers, for you have refused to obey the commands of the Lord and have worshiped the images of Baal instead. Now summon all Israel to join me at Mount Carmel, along with the 450 prophets of Baal and the 400 prophets of Asherah who are supported by Jezebel." So Ahab summoned all the people of Israel and the prophets to Mount Carmel. Then Elijah stood in front of them and said, "How much longer will you waver, hobbling between two opinions? If the Lord is God, follow him! But if Baal is God, then follow him!" But the people were completely silent* (1 Kings 18:1-2, 17-21 NLT).

The prophets of Baal danced around their altar the entire day, cutting themselves, abasing themselves, and...nothing. The gods of this world are just that—nothing. Then it was Elijah's turn, and he began to build his altar of stones:

> *He piled wood on the altar, cut the bull into pieces, and laid the pieces on the wood. Then he said, "Fill four large jars with water, and pour the water over the offering and the wood." After they had done this, he said, "Do the same thing again!" And when they were finished, he said, "Now do it a third time!" So they did as he said, and the water ran around the altar and even filled the trench. At the usual time for offering the evening sacrifice, Elijah the prophet walked up to the altar and prayed, "O Lord, God of Abraham, Isaac, and Jacob, prove today that you are God in Israel and that I am your servant. Prove that I have done all this at your command. O Lord, answer me! Answer me so these people will know that you, O Lord, are God and that you have brought them back to yourself." Immediately the fire of the Lord flashed down from heaven and burned up the young bull, the wood, the stones, and the dust. It even licked up all the water in the trench! And when all the people saw it, they fell face down on the ground and cried out, "The Lord—he is God! Yes, the Lord is God!"* (1 Kings 18:33-39 NLT).

When God moved here He moved thoroughly and completely. We must remember that when we're caught up in our own spiritual battles. God didn't just burn the sacrifice, He threw in the soaked wood, the stones, *and* the soil! To top it off, when the humiliation of the prophets of Baal was complete, "the power of the Lord came on Elijah and, tucking his cloak into his belt, he ran ahead of Ahab all the way to Jezreel" (1 Kings 18:46).

Eric Liddle, Olympic running champion in 1924, is quoted

as saying, "When I run I feel God's pleasure." That's what Elijah was feeling as he overtook Ahab and his fastest horses, running in the power of the Spirit. Elijah was not afraid of the king because he was working in God's strength. The queen was another matter; one life threat from Queen Jezebel sent him running:

> Now Ahab told Jezebel everything Elijah had done and how he had killed all the prophets with the sword. So Jezebel sent a messenger to Elijah to say, "May the gods deal with me, be it ever so severely, if by this time tomorrow I do not make your life like that of one of them." Elijah was afraid and ran for his life (1 Kings 19:1-3).

Elijah Perseveres—But this Time in His Own Strength

Elijah ran, this time in his own strength, and was left physically and emotionally depleted. A far cry from when he raced Ahab's chariot "in the power of the Lord." We can all relate to this. On a spiritual high one day, nothing can intimidate you. The next you're saying, "You know what? This is too much! It's more than I bargained for. I quit." Elijah had just experienced a massive spiritual high, but he wasn't immune from lows.

Running in his own strength, Elijah collapsed under a tree, filled with disappointment in himself and disillusionment with God. Crying out to God in fear and frustration he said, "'I have had enough, Lord....Take my life; I am no better than my ancestors'" (1 Kings 19:4).

The spiritual battle Elijah was engaged in hadn't stopped just because he was on the run. God's enemy roars like a lion and inspires fear (1 Peter 5:8). You fear most when you feel powerlessness—like Elijah at this point. Fear grips you when you're going through a crisis of faith, exactly what Elijah was going through. You feel fear when you're caught up in relationships that are going wrong. When things are out of your control, fear threatens to take over. Fear clouds your vision when you lose your focus on God and start to focus on yourself.

Elijah's fear fueled him to run for days, which took a fair amount of perseverance itself, and then continued running for over a month in the direction of Mount Horeb, the mountain of God (Exodus 3:1)—the very mountain where Moses met with God face-to-face, and where God handed down the Ten Commandments. Elijah was running away from Jezebel, but I'm not sure he was running away from God at all. I believe he was running to where he thought he would *find* God, where it had always been safe, where God had shown Himself personally to Moses years before.

When Jezebel threatened him, it started a negative chain reaction:

- Fear entered Elijah's heart.
- His fear shifted his focus and he forgot all that God had previously done for him (forgetting that he had recently told a poor widow not to be afraid, give him the last of her food, and trust God to care for her!).
- He stopped trusting God to take care of him and started taking care of himself (and got it wrong by running away).
- He left his servant behind, cutting himself off from someone who could have spoken truth about God to him and reminded him of God's past faithfulness and power.
- His physical exhaustion began a downward spiral that led to emotional and spiritual weakness, which ultimately led to doubt.
- Doubt fed untruths that Satan planted in his mind, and he was deceived into thinking he was doing a good thing.
- He *thinks* he is in God's strength because in his mind he is running *toward* God.

But God wanted Elijah in Jezreel, where he had come from, not at Mount Horeb. And so, although Elijah was looking straight ahead—although his gaze was firmly fixed—it was firmly fixed on what *Elijah* wanted, and not on what *God* wanted.

After nine years of living in Austria in a missionary team situation, my husband and I transferred to Nottingham, England. I *loved* it! All of a sudden I was a grown-up again: I was fluent in the language (as fluent as a Canadian speaking British English can be) so I could discuss things with my daughters' teachers; I could understand food labels (much to my family's relief). The biggest bonus was that I made four very good friends. After four years my husband and I decided it was necessary to move closer to London, and although I knew this was the right thing, I was absolutely devastated at the thought of leaving my friends. Then one day after having a good cry with my eight-year-old daughter, she looked up at me and said, "You know, Mommy, Nottingham has been good, but if it's not where God wants us, it won't stay good."

Mount Horeb was good, but if it wasn't where God wanted Elijah it wouldn't stay good. Jezreel, where God had originally sent him, was where God wanted to work through him, in the middle of his fear and powerlessness. In this same way God wanted David (in Part 1) back in the fields, alone with the frustration of not yet being allowed to get on with what God had anointed him to do. God sometimes allows us to be in situations of powerlessness, because it is here that we see His amazing power over circumstances.

God addresses fear head-on in the first chapter of Joshua, as the nation of Israel faced the walls of Jericho. "Fear not," He says, "be strong and very courageous." Then He goes on to say this, in the very next breath:

> *Keep this Book of the Law always on your lips; meditate on it day and night, so that you may be careful to do everything written in it. Then you will be prosperous and successful. Have I not*

> commanded you? Be strong and courageous. Do not be afraid; do not be discouraged, for the Lord your God will be with you wherever you go (Joshua 1:8-9).

In the context of fear, God's answer is: "Know Me, read about Me, know what I've done." Sometimes we know very little about the Scriptures; we need to read them, and keep reading them, both the Old Testament and the New. This is how we remind ourselves of God's power, His faithfulness, and His promises. God does not expect us to face things alone. He knows where we are in our faith journey.

How confident are you in God in the face of your fears? How confident are you that He is with you?

> When your health, your finances or family are at risk, you suddenly realise how fragile life is. Today you may be living on the sunny side of the street, but if you live long enough adversity will come knocking on your door. When it does, you'll discover that things like power, possessions and popularity won't sustain you.
>
> If power could do it, Joseph Stalin wouldn't have been afraid to go to sleep at night or been so paranoid that he appointed a soldier to guard his very teabags. If possessions could do it, fear wouldn't have caused billionaire Howard Hughes to live like a hermit and die alone. If popularity could do it, John Lennon's biographers wouldn't have described him as a fearful man who slept with the lights on and was terrified of germs.
>
> Earthly supports can only sustain you so long. Courage for living comes from a deep abiding trust in God, whose Word says, "This is the victory that has overcome the world, even our faith" [1 John 5:4]. But faith is only as

valuable as the thing it's placed in, and our faith is in a God who never fails! David said, "Through you we push back our enemies; through your name we trample our foes" (Psalm 44:5 NIV). Jesus said, "I have given you authority to... overcome all the power of the enemy..." (Luke 10:19 NIV). Paul said, "Who shall separate us from the love of Christ? Shall trouble or hardship or persecution or famine or nakedness or danger or sword?...No, in all these things we are more than conquerors through him who loved us" (Romans 8:35-37 NIV).[10]

Elijah was full of fear—a consuming, distorting fear. At this point I wonder if God wanted to just shake him! Had God not fed him, cared for him, raised a dead child for him, and killed hundreds of false prophets in answer to his prayers? Was God not big enough to protect him from one venomous woman? Fear makes the ineffectual overpowering. Fear distorts reason.

Fear is:

False
Evidence
Appearing
Real

The Apostle Paul said to a young, overwhelmed Timothy, "For the Spirit God gave us does not make us timid, but gives us power, love and self-discipline" (2 Timothy 1:7). Let's break that down:

- Power—in Jesus's name (John 14:12-14)
- Love—through Jesus's spirit (John 13:35)
- A sound mind—fear consumes and distorts, but love casts out fear (1 John 4:18)

Part 3: Perseverance

Timothy was an experienced traveler (in a time when traveling could be extremely dangerous) and this was a young man Paul trusted enough to leave in charge of church plants close to Paul's heart. This doesn't exactly describe a timid soul, rather someone who's quite courageous. On the other hand, three times Paul mentioned fear in relation to Timothy. I got a little annoyed at all the implications in various commentaries that he was a fearful, timid person. I see Timothy more as a man in conflict. Often, even those with the gift of faith experience fear when it means moving into unknown territory.

I don't imagine Paul suffered weak people gladly, so I think it's a bit unfair to paint Timothy with the brush of weakness, when actually there was more here to be fearful of than meets the eye:

- Nero—who dipped believers in tar and ignited them to provide light for midnight parties in his garden—was in power.
- Christians were being torn to shreds and eaten by wild beasts in the arena. They were being scourged, mocked, and crucified.
- Timothy was dealing with grief over knowing Paul's days were numbered; dealing with petrified believers looking to Timothy and Paul's "team" for direction; and dealing with the huge responsibility Paul was laying on him.

"God did not give you a spirit of fear, but of power, love, and a sound mind."

While writing *Guard your Heart*, the movie *The Killing Fields* came on the television. (I thought I had it on the Comedy Channel, but no.) The fear in this movie is palpable. It is real. Fear is controlling. It totally gripped me, and I was just watching a movie!

But fear is ineffectual in light of God's power. When you are in the grip of fear, most likely you are trying to work out of your own strength; and here was Elijah—burnt out, trying to carry on when he had no strength left, physically or spiritually—afraid for his life. But while Elijah slept in the desert, God cared for him:

> *Elijah was afraid and ran for his life. When he came to Beersheba in Judah, he left his servant there, while he himself went a day's journey into the wilderness. He came to a broom bush, sat down under it and prayed that he might die. "I have had enough, Lord," he said. "Take my life; I am no better than my ancestors." Then he lay down under the bush and fell asleep. All at once an angel touched him and said, "Get up and eat." He looked around, and there by his head was some bread baked over hot coals, and a jar of water. He ate and drank and then lay down again. The angel of the Lord came back a second time and touched him and said, "Get up and eat, for the journey is too much for you." So he got up and ate and drank. Strengthened by that food, he traveled forty days and forty nights until he reached Horeb, the mountain of God* (1 Kings 19:3-8).

What a powerful, but often unnoticed, testament to God's faithfulness. Even when he wasn't aware of it, God was providing for Elijah and sent an angel and food—not just once, but twice. God understands that sometimes the journey is just too much and we simply despair. When the angel of the Lord came back the second time he said, "Get up and eat, for the journey is too much for you" (1 Kings 19:7).

How many times have you felt that it's just too much? God said to me through these verses, "I know, the journey is too much for you. Take up *My* strength."

But maybe you're getting it right. Maybe you *are* waiting on God these days, you *are* obeying Him and persevering, but

PART 3: PERSEVERANCE

the journey is *still* too much, and you don't see the results you hoped for. I've felt like that. In fact, as I write this chapter it's winter and I'm sitting alone in our cold apartment in Albania. My daughters are back in England, my husband's away. I'm struggling to learn the language, unable to do much without an interpreter, and contemplating a few more years here. I sometimes find myself thinking, "I can't do this, it's too much."

In Isaiah, there is a wonderful promise: "Even youths grow tired and weary, and young men stumble and fall; but those who hope in the Lord will renew their strength. They will soar on wings like eagles; they will run and not grow weary, they will walk and not be faint" (Isaiah 40:30-31).

In his book *If You Want to Walk on Water, You've Got to Get Out of the Boat*, John Ortberg describes three methods of a bird's flight. The first is flapping—this is when a bird keeps their wings in constant motion. Hummingbirds can flap up to seventy times per second. Flapping will overcome gravity and keep a bird airborne, but it expends a lot of energy.

Next we have gliding. This is when the bird has built up enough speed that it can coast downward. To our eye, gliding is more graceful than flapping. However, birds can't travel far by this means.

Then comes the final method—soaring. Eagles are one of only a few birds able to soar. Eagles' strong wings can catching rising currents of warm air and ride them to great heights without needing to move a feather. Soaring eagles have been clocked at up to 80 mph.[11]

Elijah had been soaring, but after suffering a bit of criticism, the fear of attack knocked him right back and he was reduced to ineffectual flapping (1 Kings 19:3-8). He came to a broom tree, sat down under it, and prayed that he might die. Disappointment with himself settled in—which happens when we do things in our own strength with ourselves as the focus—and disillusionment with God was not far behind.

Elijah Persevered in the Cave: God's Power in Elijah's Weakness

Having persevered for forty days of running, Elijah ended up in a cave on Mount Horeb: "The word of God came to him: 'So Elijah, what are you doing here?' [And God was about to get an earful] 'I've been working my heart out for the God-of-the-Angel-Armies,' said Elijah. 'The people of Israel have abandoned your covenant, destroyed the places of worship, and murdered your prophets. I'm the only one left, and now they're trying to kill me'" (1 Kings 19:9-10 MSG).

We need to look at his response closely, because Elijah's response is fairly typical of what we all do when we start relying on our own strength and are challenged by God on it: a twofold response of blame shifting and believing things that are not true.

First came a bit of self-defense: "I've been working my heart out for the God-of-the-Angel-Armies" with an implied criticism that God had not done anything for him. This was not true; at the very least God had fed and given him strength supernaturally on this very journey, and there was a whole list of times prior to this that Elijah was conveniently forgetting.

Then, rather than coming right out with the fact that he was afraid, Elijah did a bit of blame shifting: "The people of Israel have abandoned your covenant, destroyed the places of worship and murdered your prophets." Again, this was not true. Just over a month before when Elijah stood before the nation of Israel and the fire of the Lord burned up the sacrifice—along with the wood, the stones, the soil, and even the water in the ditch around the altar—he himself was a witness to the fact that, "When all the people saw this, they fell prostrate and cried, 'The Lord—he is God! The Lord—he is God!'" (1 Kings 18:39).

And finally: "I am the only one left." Which again was not true; there were 7000 who had not bowed down to Baal (19:18). Elijah himself had engaged in a lengthy conversation with the prophet Obadiah in chapter 18. And, in addition, God had a younger prophet Elisha raised up and waiting.

This is what fear does—it opens us up to believing untruths, and untruths can lead us into making decisions and choices that are not at all in line with God's will for us. Neil Anderson, in his book *The Bondage Breaker,* describes truth as "a battle for the mind."[12] Satan suggests the untruth, with just enough plausibility or containing enough truth to make it seem unarguable.

Satan planted the lie in my mind that because I felt unwanted in my family then God didn't really want me either. Of course I could be a Christian because Jesus died on the cross for this, but as far as *really* being a part of the family, well there was no chance of that type of acceptance. Was that the truth? No. Did that lie affect my life, decisions, and choices for forty-two years? Yes. It wasn't until I acknowledged this, confessed it, turned away from it, and began speaking the truth, that I was freed from the lies and the fear that accompanied them.

If you believe a lie, it affects your life, no matter what the lie is, and this was happening with Elijah. He began believing a string of untruths, initiated by Jezebel's threat; but God doesn't engage in conversation here. He simply says:

> *"Go out and stand on the mountain in the presence of the Lord, for the Lord is about to pass by." Then a great and powerful wind tore the mountains apart and shattered the rocks before the Lord, but the Lord was not in the wind. After the wind there was an earthquake, but the Lord was not in the earthquake. After the earthquake came a fire, but the Lord was not in the fire. And after the fire came a gentle whisper* (1 Kings 19:11-12).

Elijah *did* step outside the cave; and to his credit, he didn't go back in. Not one of those experiences of perseverance was easy. I imagine each was downright frightening. The secret of persevering is not being the self-sufficient, controlling, tough one. Tough people look at themselves, weak people look at Jesus. Remember, 2 Corinthians 12:9 says, "But [God] said to me [the Apostle Paul], 'My grace is sufficient for you, for my power is made perfect in weakness.'" The Bible does not only praise great faith, the Bible praises simple faith (Luke 18:17 TLB).

- **Elijah persevered through the hurricane.** My sister lives in North Carolina on the Atlantic coast, and she understands living through a hurricane. It's devastating and destructive, it rips trees out of the ground, flattens houses, wrecks everything it touches, throws things into chaos. Hurricanes leave people in turmoil. What leaves *you* in turmoil—circumstances, people, relationships broken in a maelstrom of abuse?
- **He persevered through the earthquake.** Earthquakes shake your foundation, shake up everything you put your confidence in. Where do you find your security? On what are you building the foundations of your life—in material things, a job, education, your family? And, more importantly, what will your confidence be grounded in *after* the earthquake?
- **He persevered through the fire.** Fire destroys whatever the hurricane and earthquake leave behind. It leaves you completely destitute, with only your memories. What a picture of the trials Elijah just lived through.

But because he persevered, Elijah heard God's voice gently asking the same question again, *"What are you doing here?"* Yet there is no anger, no recriminations, no blaming, no condemning—just the one question.

Here was Elijah's choice: He could stay in the cave, telling himself untruths, or he could step outside the cave, as God told him to do, and deal with the situation in the light of God's truth and strength.

And here is our choice: We can stay in the cave, telling ourselves untruths, or we can step outside the cave, as God urges us to do, and deal with the situation in the light of His truth and strength. We may not understand, but we trust in our God's love and goodness; that's when we stand on the *rock* of our faith. And our hearts are guarded. Eyes looking straight ahead, fixed on God and finding our strength in Him.

We may be running, thinking we are running toward God, where we have found Him safely in the past. But we are actually running away from where God *really* wants us, where there may be threats, disappointment, disillusionment, and powerlessness. It is when we are in these places that God's power will be seen—not inside the safe cave, but out on the ledge.

Perseverance Brought an Unexpected Response

Elijah had run to where he knew he would find God, and he did find Him, but he didn't get the answer he was expecting. God challenged Elijah to take courage, to come out of the cave and go back to Jezreel, where Jezebel was, where his fear had taken hold and where the running began. How mortifying *that* was going to be! Elijah had run away in fear and shame, and God was sending him back to the scene of his humiliation, to the queen who was looking to kill him, because God had things for Elijah to do. Note that again there was no rebuke, no words of condemnation, just God urging Elijah not to stay where he was. It required repentance and humility on Elijah's part to go back. It may require repentance and humility for us, but we won't be the first:

- Moses was a murderer hiding in a desert for forty years,

hiding from his past, and God came to him with the same instructions: "So now, go. I am sending you to Pharaoh to bring my people the Israelites out of Egypt" (Exodus 3:10). I have something for you to do!

- Peter had been on a spiritual high for three years living and serving with Jesus, but then denied even knowing Him three times. He ran back to his boat, where it was familiar, to start over—disappointed and disillusioned. Jesus found him, looked Peter in the eye, and said: "Feed my sheep" (John 21:17). I have something for you to do!

- Hagar was a young, pregnant slave girl who was running away from her situation at home. This is a piece of her story, where God told her to go back: "Then Sarai mistreated Hagar; so she fled from her. The angel of the Lord found Hagar near a spring in the desert; it was the spring that is beside the road to Shur. And he said, 'Hagar, slave of Sarai, where have you come from, and where are you going?' 'I'm running away from my mistress Sarai,' she answered. Then the angel of the Lord told her, 'Go back to your mistress and submit to her.' The angel added, 'I will increase your descendants so much that they will be too numerous to count'" (Genesis 16:6-10). I have something for you to do!

We often think it best to leave our circumstances, but God sometimes says, "Stay and see me work through you."

Let me say here that there are cases where it is dangerous to stay or return to an abusive situation, and in these cases, you need to get help. But for most of us, God wants to work *in* the situation, and we need to remember and focus on the facts that God is good, God is faithful, and God's power is there in our weakness.

My husband Brian and I spend several weeks a year in Cambodia. There we met a young man named Hem Chanthorn. Chanthorn had been part of the local mafia when he was led to the Lord by his wife. Consequently, he had been severely persecuted for his faith, put in a cage in the town center for entire days in the heat with no food or water. Not long after this, Chanthorn asked his pastor and Brian to baptize him because he felt God telling him to *go back* to the place where he had been persecuted and plant a church. It was a humiliating thing to do, to go back where people had publicly mocked him, and where he might yet be martyred for his faith. It took courage, perseverance, and simple faith. I say "simple faith" because that's exactly what Chanthorn's faith is: He believes God is who He says He is, and does what He says He will do. Simple. We don't need enormous faith. Jesus tells us we only need a mustard seed of faith in order to move mountains (Matthew 17:20). Great faith grows out of simple faith.

God keeps His promise to go with us, and Chanthorn has planted a church—in fact he has now planted two!

I wonder if Chanthorn felt fear at the thought of going back. Fear not just for himself, but for his wife and their two little boys who went with him. I wonder if Satan tried to convince him to stay safe in the town of Possat (his cave). Possibly it's fear that is going to keep you in your cave. Where does that fear come from? Is embarrassment or humiliation the basis for it? Maybe it is some*one* you are afraid of, maybe you are even afraid of God.

Proverbs 4:24-25 (NASB) says, "Put away from you a deceitful mouth"—stop telling yourself untruths—"Let your eyes look directly ahead." Go back to the point from where you ran from God, the point that so filled you with fear that you couldn't see Him there straight in front of you. Look honestly at your disappointment and disillusionment and ask God to show you His perspective. This time be ready to hear it and respond.

Elijah began by persevering with faithful obedience every time and (after some drama) obediently going back to where God wanted him, humbling himself in the process. His life ended when he was taken into heaven in a whirlwind, leaving the legacy of a young prophet God gave him to mentor named Elisha, who became one of God's greatest prophets ever.

GUARD YOUR HEART — AUDREY PHILLIPS JOSE

When you guard your heart by persevering in obedience, there is no doubt about it—you *will* leave a legacy for God's kingdom, and you *will* experience the power of God along the way.

PART 3: PERSEVERANCE

Perseverance

1. **Read Psalm 40.**
   Underline, circle, or mark the text that speaks to you.

   I waited patiently for the Lord;
      he turned to me and heard my cry.
   ² He lifted me out of the slimy pit,
      out of the mud and mire;
   he set my feet on a rock
      and gave me a firm place to stand.
   ³ He put a new song in my mouth,
      a hymn of praise to our God.
   Many will see and fear the Lord
      and put their trust in him.

   ⁴ Blessed is the one
      who trusts in the Lord,
   who does not look to the proud,
      to those who turn aside to false gods.
   ⁵ Many, Lord my God,
      are the wonders you have done,
      the things you planned for us.
   None can compare with you;
      were I to speak and tell of your deeds,
      they would be too many to declare.

   ⁶ Sacrifice and offering you did not desire—
      but my ears you have opened—
      burnt offerings and sin offerings you did not require.
   ⁷ Then I said, "Here I am, I have come—
      it is written about me in the scroll.
   ⁸ I desire to do your will, my God;
      your law is within my heart."

   ⁹ I proclaim your saving acts in the great assembly;
      I do not seal my lips, Lord,
      as you know.
   ¹⁰ I do not hide your righteousness in my heart;
      I speak of your faithfulness and your saving help.
   I do not conceal your love and your faithfulness

from the great assembly.

¹¹ Do not withhold your mercy from me, Lord;
  may your love and faithfulness always protect me.
¹² For troubles without number surround me;
  my sins have overtaken me, and I cannot see.
They are more than the hairs of my head,
  and my heart fails within me.
¹³ Be pleased to save me, Lord;
  come quickly, Lord, to help me.

¹⁴ May all who want to take my life
  be put to shame and confusion;
may all who desire my ruin
  be turned back in disgrace.
¹⁵ May those who say to me, "Aha! Aha!"
  be appalled at their own shame.
¹⁶ But may all who seek you
  rejoice and be glad in you;
may those who long for your saving help always say,
  "The Lord is great!"

¹⁷ But as for me, I am poor and needy;
  may the Lord think of me.
You are my help and my deliverer;
  you are my God, do not delay.

2. What does it say?
Make a verse-by-verse list of the most outstanding, obvious facts. Do not paraphrase—*just use words in the text.*

3. What does it mean?

Part 3: Perseverance

What spiritual lessons or principles can be learned from these facts?

4. Now, what does it mean in my life?
Rewrite the lessons/principles from Step 3 in the form of a personal question.

PART 4

PRAYER

Make level paths for your feet and take only ways that are firm (Proverbs 4:26).

In the 1980s, my husband and I were on a team that smuggled Bibles into former Communist Eastern Europe. In order to maximize space and get as many Bibles as possible into limited areas, a mantra was drilled into us from day 1: ALWAYS START WITH A LEVEL BASE. That wasn't easy because the spaces were in very awkward places. However, if you started with a level base you could get a lot more Bibles packed in than if you just rammed them in any old way.

This verse in Proverbs instructs us to "Make level paths for your feet"—start with a level base by removing stones on the path. Stones of hopelessness, powerlessness, hate, bitterness, despair, temptation, work, "things," sometimes even people. Stones such as these (and notice not all of them are sinful in and of themselves) can trip you up and cause you to stumble or make detours in your Christian walk.

"And take only ways that are firm." Ways that are firm provide security, assurance, and confidence. Ways that are firm involve grace, truth, faithfulness, love, and hope, and require some action by us.

I recently read about a woman whose path had become littered with stones. Her husband was ill and lost his job. In the financial crisis of 2009 they lost their home. They had five children to provide for. She tried to find work, but the situation continued to worsen.

One day she became so desperate and her life seemed so hopeless that she took her little girl into the bedroom, covered the windows and turned on the gas heater without lighting it. The stones in her life had become boulders. They had tripped her up one too many times, and she could no longer see a way to get past them.

As the gas slowly filled the room, she heard someone singing these words from an old hymn: "Oh what peace we often forfeit, oh what needless pain we bear; all because we do not carry, everything to God in prayer." She had inadvertently left the radio on, but it saved her life. Those words went straight to her heart. She turned off the gas and began to pray, this time not focusing on the insurmountable boulders in her life, but instead taking her crushing burden to God and turning her prayer into one of thanksgiving.

Prayer changes your perspective, and what had seemed like overwhelming boulders were merely pebbles in God's hands.

What are the stones in your life that need to be removed? Financial worries? A rebellious child? A loved one with dementia? Illness? Where do you need to make a level path in your walk with God by bringing every rock, stone, boulder, dead root, or piece of litter to Him?

Joseph is a great example of someone who guarded his heard by making a level path in his walk with God, which in turn guarded his heart from anger, regret, and bitterness.

The story of Joseph begins in Genesis 30, and although he was his father's favorite son among his 10 brothers, a young Joseph's life graph would have been on a steady downward slide, punctuated with incidents of betrayal from family and friends:

- He was subjected to hatred and rejection at the hand of his brothers while in his father's home.
- He endured a terrifying journey to a foreign country,

the result of betrayal by his brothers.
- He stood on the slave block until he was sold to Potiphar, a demeaning and humiliating experience.
- He was put in charge of Potiphar's household. A short-lived upward turn, until he was put in prison because of the lies of a vindictive woman, a betrayal by someone who had no cause to hurt him.
- Friends he made in prison and who promised to mention his case to Pharaoh but "forgot." The result of this betrayal meant he endured two more years in prison.

And he wasn't even thirty yet! (Genesis 41:46)

Make a Level Path by Recognizing and Removing Stones that Make You Stumble

Joseph spent his life removing stones and boulders from his life's path: a stone of self-importance after his dreams (Genesis 37:7-10); the stone of sexual temptation (Genesis 39:6-12); as well as stones of bitterness, betrayal, and huge "what if" boulders of past mistakes and regrets. Temptation to have pride in the positions awarded him could have been another stone in his path. Other stones might have been anger, despair, and depression. I suspect one of the biggest boulders he had to deal with was to forgive—not only his brothers who betrayed him, but also Potiphar's wife who lied about him, Potiphar who turned against him, and his two friends in jail who used him and forgot about their promises to him.

Somehow Joseph managed to remove the boulder of unforgiveness over the course of his life. How do we know this? Because twenty years after being sold as a slave by his brothers, and after twenty years of massive ups and downs in his life, Joseph said this to them: "You intended to harm me, but God intended it for good to accomplish what is now being done, the saving of many lives" (Genesis 50:20).

How was Joseph able to react with grace toward his brothers instead of with hostility and revenge? I believe it was because during all those lonely years in a foreign country, separated from his family, he had learned to call upon God's presence through prayer, thus removing stones to make a level path for himself. The result was an increase of God's grace in his life—and grace goes hand-in-hand with forgiveness. He began learning this in his late teens when his brothers betrayed him and he found himself on a journey that would change the course of his life forever.

As with Daniel in Part 2, when Joseph was sold by his brothers he was probably stripped even of his clothing, tied to the men in front and behind him, and walked all the way to Egypt. Unlike Daniel, it was his own family who had betrayed him. I have sometimes wondered which hurt most, the physical hardships of his journey and subsequent servitude, or the betrayal by family members he trusted.

With every step Joseph took away from his home and spiritual comfort zone, he was constantly challenged to make level paths for his feet and take only ways that were firm. Satan was right there, with every painful step, urging him to question everything he had been taught about God, especially His goodness—because a good God wouldn't have let this happen, would He? Questioning God's goodness is the first step to faltering in your prayer life, tripping yourself up over pebbles, stones, or boulders of doubt.

There is a term in psychology called "learned helplessness."[13] It is the giving-up reaction, the quitting response that follows from the belief that *whatever you do doesn't matter*. For someone in Joseph's position, first as a slave, then abandoned in prison for years, it would be very easy to fall into this pattern of thinking. He couldn't seem to get ahead, and even his God-given gifts and talents seemed to backfire on him!

Part 4: Prayer

Make a Level Path by Asking God to Show You His Perspective

The life of Joseph, told in Genesis chapters 37-50, is an example of finding a way to live with the consequences of someone else's sin without it becoming a stone of bondage to bitterness in your path. When Joseph confronted his brothers with the words, "You intended to harm me," his rebuke is short and to the point. The guilt is set squarely on the shoulders of those responsible. "But God" is the key phrase, the underlying rock of Joseph's faith. Two little words that kept him going despite several horrific years, and that reveal the true nature of Joseph's heart.

If anyone learned the secret of seeing things from God's perspective, this man did. It had been just him and God for many years. Six times in two chapters we read, "But the Lord was with Joseph and extended kindness to him." That simply does not happen when our hearts are in rebellion or we're shaking our fist at God.

This was Joseph's secret. He became the man that he was, who saw God in the big picture, because he had forgiven his brothers even though they never asked for his forgiveness.

At some point Joseph stopped asking "Why?" and started asking "For what purpose?" There is a huge difference between these two questions. "Why" is self-oriented—why is this happening *to me*; why have you done this *to me*—and demands justification. "For what purpose" acknowledges God's greater plan, and invites dialogue with Him to reveal it.

Prayer is the key that lets the supernatural power of God break into the lives of ordinary people: "For our struggle is not against flesh and blood, but against...the powers of this dark world. With this in mind...always keep on praying" (Ephesians 6:12, 18).

Don't just pray that God will solve problems or take away difficulties. Pray that God will reveal Himself *in* the difficulty.

Pray for spiritual growth as a result of the problems. Pray the life-changing power of the Holy Spirit into the situation. Scheming, manipulating, railing against circumstances are not effective means of "waiting on the Lord."

> Don't just pray that God will solve problems or take away difficulties. Pray that God will reveal Himself IN the difficulties.

My own experience has taught me that you cannot have a dynamic prayer life if you're harboring unforgiveness toward someone. This is not to minimize in any way anything that may have happened to you. Jesus Himself said that some people deserve to have a large millstone hung around their neck and to be drowned in the depths of the sea (Matthew 18:6). Some people *won't care* if you have forgiven them or not. What you have to realize is that *forgiveness is for you.* Not for anyone else. It's between you and God. Forgiveness doesn't excuse an abuser; forgiveness frees you. When you yourself are freed through forgiveness, it evokes in you a response of worship to the Lord who has forgiven you more than you have ever had to forgive anyone else.

We often equate forgiveness with saying, "It no longer matters," or what my mom used to say, "Never mind." That is not at all what it means. In fact there are a few more things that forgiveness is not:

- It does *not* mean you tolerate sin.
- It is *not* denying our feelings of anger, sadness, or betrayal.
- It is *not* an easy, superficial response that removes the need to face things honestly.

Forgiveness is finding a way to live with the consequences

of another person's sin without seeking revenge or repayment. With regard to our own sin, God does not pretend it did not happen. He does not tolerate it. He has provided a way to deal with it—the cross. And He forgives it.

A story I came across tells about two friends who were walking through the desert. At some point of the journey, they had an argument, and one friend slapped the other one in the face. The one who got slapped was hurt, but without saying anything, he wrote in the sand: TODAY MY BEST FRIEND SLAPPED ME IN THE FACE.

They kept on walking until they found an oasis, where they decided to take a bath. The one who had been slapped got stuck in the mire and started drowning, but his friend saved him. After he recovered from the near drowning, he wrote on a stone: TODAY MY BEST FRIEND SAVED MY LIFE.

The friend, who had both slapped and saved his best friend, asked him, "After I hurt you, you wrote in the sand, and now, you write on a stone. Why?"

The other friend replied, "When someone hurts us, we should write it down in sand, where the winds of forgiveness can erase it away, but when someone does something good for us, we must engrave it in stone where no wind can ever erase it. Learn to write your hurts in the sand and to carve your blessings in stone."[14]

Satan wants to hurt you. He does not want you to grow in Christ, and the last thing he wants you to do is to grasp the concept of forgiveness. He wants you bound by bitterness and anger at the evil done against you. He wants you to believe that you have to do something to get back at that person.

Forgiveness is laying the blood of Jesus over the sin against you and giving Him the grief and pain.[15] It is when you are unwilling to forgive that problems start because it puts up a barrier between you and God. With Joseph's life we learn that it's not an "I forgive you and it's over" thing; forgiveness will possibly take a long time, but we have to *be open* to it. Only the Holy Spirit can bring about true forgiveness, so we shouldn't feel guilty when we can't forgive on our own accord. We can't because we have memories that make it impossible to forget the sin against us.

Let me share one thing I have started doing on my own road to forgiving someone who sinned (and is still sinning) against me. Knowing I couldn't pray for this person with 100% sincerity—and knowing it would eventually stunt my own spiritual growth if I couldn't get past this—I decided to pray one of Paul's prayers; after all, he has some pretty good ones. I set about reading through his letters, and came across:

- *"I always thank God for you."* Er, no, I couldn't pray that.
- *"I have not stopped thanking God for you."* Nix.
- *"I always pray with joy because of our partnership."* Certainly not.
- *"I long to see you that I may be filled with joy."* Is Paul nuts?

Then I found this in Colossians: "We continually ask God to fill you with the knowledge of his will through all the wisdom and understanding that the Spirit gives, so that you may live a life worthy of the Lord and please him in every way: bearing fruit in every good work, growing in the knowledge of God" (Colossians 1:9-10). This I could pray and actually mean it.

Praying that the person who betrayed me would come to a knowledge of Christ that would transform their life has leveled out this piece of the road for me, removing the stones that Satan is constantly throwing in my path with relation to this issue. It has proven to me that when you are praying for someone, you cannot hold on to bitterness, resentment, and unforgiveness.

Make a Level Path by Recognizing God's Presence in Every Circumstance of Your Life

Part 4: Prayer

Joseph's was a life full of stumbling stones to his faith, with boulders that would crush anyone's spirit, but he saw God's presence everywhere that he was. Joseph had learned that prayer—*with thanksgiving*—in every care, anxiety, and need of life is the means God has appointed for us to obtain freedom from all anxiety, and replacing it with the peace of God which passes all understanding (Philippians 4:6-7).

Joseph's past had no pull on him; his future was before him, bad or good (and with his record, that wasn't a sure thing!), but it was a future entrusted completely to God. However, in-between the past and the future is *now*. What are you filling your "now" with? What did Joseph fill his "now" with? Did he fill it with scheming, manipulating, railing against circumstances, asking why the long delay in getting him out of prison? Asking why God couldn't have intervened *before* it all happened?

No. Joseph saw God's hand everywhere. His life graph was pretty disheartening, but he saw God in the happenings of every day, and it changed his perspective for life.

I have a friend with two teenagers just starting to stand on their own faith. My friend was diagnosed with cancer. Here is a beautiful quote from her journal a month into her "Why is this happening to me?" ordeal:

> "Living in the moment...this is my key to survival. In the midst of the struggle of trying to understand what is wrong inside my body, God is there soothing me. In the painful MRI, God is there comforting me. Through my friends, I see God loving me. Through the elders coming to pray over me, I see God's deep grace covering me like a warm quilt. In all the tasks I see my loving family doing for me, I see God holding me ever so gently, loving me securely. If I don't live in the moment with God, I miss the hope and security that He gives. It means I would have to face the huge hurdles alone. I cannot imagine doing this. So I seek out God. I long after Him.

And He is faithful and ever present."[16]

It can be so easy not to see God in our difficult circumstances, but here is a woman who has learned Joseph's secrets—guarding her heart against anger and bitterness at her situation by looking for God's presence, persevering, perfecting her faith through prayer, and cultivating a kingdom perspective. She made a choice to see God, to ask Him to reveal Himself to her in her physical, emotional, and spiritual pain, and God enveloped her in His work of perfecting her.

Make a Level Path by Waiting on the Lord Through Prayer

At some point early in Joseph's ordeal he must have had a heart-to-heart with God and made the choice to forgive his brothers. Forgiveness is primarily between you and God. It is releasing your need for revenge. We don't know whether it was on the road to Egypt, in Potiphar's house, or during his years in prison, but you do not develop the character Joseph had of grace and forgiveness if you are harboring bitterness and unforgiveness in your heart. It was a forgiveness only he and God knew about; his brothers certainly didn't know. In fact, they didn't even know he was alive! Joseph had a lot of time to look long and hard at himself, starting from the minute he was thrown into a pit, and he had to make a choice: to live a life of bitterness seeking revenge; or to live by a set of standards that honored God, to set his feet on a level, firm path by asking, "For what purpose, Lord?"

There came a time in Egypt, seven years before the famine, when Joseph had power, position, and money—and he knew where his family lived. He could have had his brothers slaughtered or he could have contacted them and told them where he was and that he was safe. He didn't do either. Quite possibly he simply wasn't ready to. It was a long time before he voiced his feelings to his brothers, made himself vulnerable to those who had hurt him so deeply.

There are two great truths here: Prayer leads to forgiveness, and prayer (waiting on the Lord) will transform your life, because you will no longer have a need for revenge. Time and time again when I would be praying about my own situation, I wanted to pray some of David's prayers of vengeance on his enemies (which initially I did!) but I kept coming across verses such as:

- "Wait for the Lord; be strong and take heart and wait for the Lord" (Psalm 27:14).
- "We wait in hope for the Lord; he is our help and our shield. In him our hearts rejoice, for we trust in his holy name. May your unfailing love be with us, Lord, even as we put our hope in you" (Psalm 33:20-22).
- "Be still before the Lord and wait patiently for him; do not fret when people succeed in their ways, when they carry out their wicked schemes" (Psalm 37:7).
- "Out of the depths I cry to You, Lord; Lord, hear my voice. Let your ears be attentive to my cry for mercy. If you, Lord, kept a record of sins, Lord, who could stand? But with you there is forgiveness, so that we can, with reverence, serve you. I wait for the Lord, my whole being waits, and in his word I put my hope" (Psalm 130:1-5).

Joseph waited. And waited. And waited. But what does "waiting on the Lord" mean exactly? It's not the passive, inactive waiting that we often think of. "Waiting on the Lord" doesn't mean we sit around idle and refuse to take responsibility. Instead, it's an active clinging to God. It's trusting Him every day, obeying him, even when things aren't going the way we want.

Waiting is hard for modern society. Used to instant gratification, we don't even like to wait for physical mail to arrive, much less spend weeks, months, or years waiting on the Lord to answer a prayer.

Are you a person who knows how to wait? I know I struggle with this. Some waiting—what I call "inconvenience waiting"—afflicts us on a daily basis, but at the end of the day, it hasn't affected us too much. In his book *If You Want to Walk on Water, You Have to Get Out of the Boat*, Ortberg talks about other kinds of waiting—serious and difficult waiting. He supplied a list of serious and difficult waitings, but let's make our own list, shall we?

- Waiting on God to move mountains and intervene in what seems like a hopeless situation.
- Waiting to die as cancer spreads.
- Waiting for the sun to rise because the darkness makes the loneliness worse.
- Waiting for a neglectful spouse to turn a kind word your way.
- Waiting nine months to hold your baby.
- Waiting for physical ailments to end or emotional trauma to heal.
- Waiting for the broken pieces of your heart to mend.

We all have to learn to wait. And for some of us, that's the hardest thing God can ask us to do. It's frustrating to open up the Bible and see the Lord instructing us to do just that.

"Suffering produces perseverance; perseverance, character; and character, hope" (Romans 5:3-4). God is the author of these characteristics, and it is through seasons of waiting that they are harvested within us and we become who God wants us to be.

> *"Commit your way to the Lord; trust in him and he will do this: He will make your righteous reward shine like the dawn, your vindication like the noonday sun. Be still before the Lord and wait patiently for him; do not fret when people succeed in their ways, when they carry*

PART 4: PRAYER

out their wicked schemes" (Psalm 37:5-7).

If the Psalms had been written in Joseph's day, I imagine this one would have been close to his heart, giving him hope whilst he waited on the Lord. And in that waiting, I imagine Joseph drawing close to Him through hours of two-way prayer.

Joseph waited on the Lord when he was first taken as a slave and let Him use him as a witness in the house of Potiphar, as a witness to prisoners, and as a witness to Pharaoh himself (Genesis 39-41). Waiting on the Lord requires trust, saying, "I will trust that God has good reasons for saying, 'Wait.' I will remember that things look different to God because He views things from an eternal perspective."

Through his waiting Joseph was being perfected. We often ignore verses on perfection, thinking it will never happen for us since only God is perfect, only Jesus could live a perfect life. Yes this is true, but you cannot get away from Paul's instructions to "strive for perfection" (2 Corinthians 13:11 GNT), and waiting on the Lord as Joseph did will bring you to this.

I have a lovely paper maché lacquered box from Russia. First, the form of the box was made out of thick paper, the design painstakingly painted on. Then it received a coat of lacquer, and another...and another—nine coats of lacquer in all until the finished product was perfect. Each successive layer needed time to harden so it could clarify and bring shine to the finished product. Each coat of lacquer had to be smoothed so there was no blemish to damage the end result and the next layer would look better than the layer before.

The creator of this little box could have stopped after painting it and slapping on a coat of lacquer, and it would have looked fine. He could have stopped with two or three layers of lacquer, and it would have looked great. But nine layers made it perfect. The key to the loveliness of this box is that there was a smooth, level base with no flecks of dust or grit to throw everything off. It took patience and a lot of waiting between each layer in order to perfect the product.

There was a lot of waiting in Joseph's life and the need for much patience; but as Joseph focused on his Lord, waiting on His timing, he was making his way level so God could build on it. His level path meant that he was able to live with the consequences of others' sin without the stones of bitterness and questioning God's provision and goodness. When Joseph refused to avenge himself, he opened channels of prayer that would affect his life forever.

The names Joseph gave his sons during these years are hugely significant and reiterate his acknowledgment that God showed grace to him. He'd had years in prison to replay the video to remind himself over and over what happened, to dwell on it, to work through his feelings, and to cry out to the Lord.

Joseph named his firstborn Manasseh, which means "making to forget." Forget means "the debt is canceled." We cannot forgive in our own strength. What Joseph said indicates his spiritual condition: "God has made me forget all my trouble and all my father's household" (Genesis 41:51). He did not pretend that his past had not caused pain, and the very fact that he named his son "Forget" indicated that there was still something he was reminding himself to forget, but he refused to take revenge, or let it control him.

My own difficult past controlled me for nineteen years as a Christian because not only could I not forget, but I couldn't forgive. I couldn't forgive others, and I especially couldn't forgive myself. You know the expression "forgive and forget"? To me it meant if I hadn't forgotten, then I hadn't forgiven. (How does one go about forgetting?) And therefore, by *not* forgetting, I was sinning somehow. Joseph got it right because every time he called his little boy he was reminding himself that *God was making him forget*—release; let go; freeing up the channel of communication between himself and God. If you have not forgiven, you cannot forget, release, or let go.

His second son he named Ephraim, meaning "fruitfulness," and this is what he said: "It is because God has made me fruitful in the land of my suffering" (Genesis 41:52). Joseph was still homesick. He still yearned for his family. He saw his time in Egypt, blessed as it had been, as an affliction, something he wished he didn't have to bear. But he was acknowledging through the name Ephraim that the reality of the affliction was softened by the goodness of God as He made Joseph fruitful.

When you look at your own story, see where you can find God. (Maybe go over your life graph with a different color pen, marking the times where you were aware of God's presence—you might be surprised at what you discover.) This is not to minimize your pain, but to have hope in the redemptive plan of God. In our culture of instant gratification we don't often take time to do this. It may encourage you to know that this was a twenty-year journey for Joseph. This is so important! God doesn't expect us to say, "Voilà" and all is forgiven. He understands the pain. He knows the impossibility of the task. But He also knows the power of prayer. *Satan* knows the power of prayer. Satan wants you in a prayer-less state. When there is an area of unforgiveness in your life, consider whether or not you're praying for that person, thereby hindering or delaying the healing process.

One of the names of God is Yahweh-Raphe. It means "the God who heals." Usually we think of God healing our physical problems. But God is the healer of much more than that. He is the healer of wounded people and broken hearts.

> If you have not forgiven, you cannot forget, release, or let go.

I have a friend who has many conflicts in her marriage. As we talked one day, it became apparent that most of the conflict originated in her own mind, and grew throughout the day until she was in battle mode by the time her husband got home. In one sentence she told me how desperately she wanted her marriage to work, the next sentence was a litany of her husband's wrongs against her. As she talked, her resentment built, and it was obvious that this wasn't the first time my friend had gone through this routine. Prayer had taken a backseat to bitterness, because she could not have a dynamic prayer life if she was harboring unforgiveness toward someone.

If you have been betrayed or hurt, you want justice, not forgiveness. Forgiveness doesn't come naturally. Joseph understood this, and as a result was neither destroyed by the things that he endured, nor by resentment that might have been attached to them. Take each thing that has offended you—each thing that has hurt you, every conflict—and lay them at the foot of the cross.

"Make level paths for your feet and take only ways that are firm. Examine yourselves, to see whether you are in the faith. Pray for perfection." How could Joseph do this?

- He practiced the presence of God in his life by acknowledging God's control.
- He chose to live a life of purity, no matter what the cost—even prison.
- He persevered and saw God's power in his weakness day after long, lonely day.
- He made choices, and the underpinning of each choice was seeking to see where God had shown grace to him.
- He cultivated an open, prayerful communication with God that transformed his life.

In doing these things he guarded his heart and was able to view events through God's perspective, and they could no longer destroy him. There came a time early on in his years in Egypt where the outcome could have been entirely different. We read his story and know the ending. When Joseph landed at Potiphar's house in his late teens, he didn't know the outcome—but he knew his God. Joseph's forgiveness, the result of hours of prayer spent in the presence of his God, enabled reconciliation, a restored relationship that his brothers didn't deserve.

Don't just pray that God will solve problems or take away

Part 4: Prayer

difficulties. Pray that God will reveal Himself *in* the difficulty. Pray for growth as the result of the problems. Pray the life-changing power of the Holy Spirit into the situation. Pray cleansing and forgiveness into the lives of those who hurt you. In all your prayers, mirror Christ, the One who can meet every need. Scheming, manipulating, railing against circumstances are not effective means of "waiting on the Lord."

Joseph began as someone with God-given gifts who didn't always handle them well. He lived a life that mirrored that of Jesus: lavishing all the good things he had on his brothers; grieving over wasted years of rejection that could have been spent in relationship with them; standing at the head of a banqueting table; extending his arms wide, revealing himself as "I am he." He ended by living the way of the cross: offering forgiveness and a new life of peace.

Prayer

1. **Read Psalm 37.**
   Underline, circle, or mark the text that speaks to you.

   Do not fret because of those who are evil
     or be envious of those who do wrong;
   2 for like the grass they will soon wither,
     like green plants they will soon die away.

   3 Trust in the Lord and do good;
     dwell in the land and enjoy safe pasture.
   4 Take delight in the Lord,
     and he will give you the desires of your heart.

   5 Commit your way to the Lord;
     trust in him and he will do this:
   6 He will make your righteous reward shine like the dawn,
     your vindication like the noonday sun.

   7 Be still before the Lord
     and wait patiently for him;
   do not fret when people succeed in their ways,
     when they carry out their wicked schemes.

   8 Refrain from anger and turn from wrath;
     do not fret—it leads only to evil.
   9 For those who are evil will be destroyed,
     but those who hope in the Lord will inherit the land.

   10 A little while, and the wicked will be no more;
     though you look for them, they will not be found.
   11 But the meek will inherit the land
     and enjoy peace and prosperity.

   12 The wicked plot against the righteous
     and gnash their teeth at them;
   13 but the Lord laughs at the wicked,
     for he knows their day is coming.

14 The wicked draw the sword
    and bend the bow
to bring down the poor and needy,
    to slay those whose ways are upright.
15 But their swords will pierce their own hearts,
    and their bows will be broken.

16 Better the little that the righteous have
    than the wealth of many wicked;
17 for the power of the wicked will be broken,
    but the Lord upholds the righteous.

18 The blameless spend their days under the Lord's care,
    and their inheritance will endure forever.
19 In times of disaster they will not wither;
    in days of famine they will enjoy plenty.

20 But the wicked will perish:
    Though the Lord's enemies are like the flowers of the field,
    they will be consumed, they will go up in smoke.

21 The wicked borrow and do not repay,
    but the righteous give generously;
22 those the Lord blesses will inherit the land,
    but those he curses will be destroyed.

23 The Lord makes firm the steps
    of the one who delights in him;
24 though he may stumble, he will not fall,
    for the Lord upholds him with his hand.

25 I was young and now I am old,
    yet I have never seen the righteous forsaken
    or their children begging bread.
26 They are always generous and lend freely;
    their children will be a blessing.

27 Turn from evil and do good;
    then you will dwell in the land forever.
28 For the Lord loves the just

and will not forsake his faithful ones.

Wrongdoers will be completely destroyed;
    the offspring of the wicked will perish.
29 The righteous will inherit the land
    and dwell in it forever.

30 The mouths of the righteous utter wisdom,
    and their tongues speak what is just.
31 The law of their God is in their hearts;
    their feet do not slip.

32 The wicked lie in wait for the righteous,
    intent on putting them to death;
33 but the Lord will not leave them in the power of the wicked
    or let them be condemned when brought to trial.

34 Hope in the Lord
    and keep his way.
He will exalt you to inherit the land;
    when the wicked are destroyed, you will see it.

35 I have seen a wicked and ruthless man
    flourishing like a luxuriant native tree,
36 but he soon passed away and was no more;
    though I looked for him, he could not be found.

37 Consider the blameless, observe the upright;
    a future awaits those who seek peace.
38 But all sinners will be destroyed;
    there will be no future for the wicked.

39 The salvation of the righteous comes from the Lord;
    he is their stronghold in time of trouble.
40 The Lord helps them and delivers them;
    he delivers them from the wicked and saves them,
    because they take refuge in him.

2. What does it say?
Make a verse-by-verse list of the most outstanding, obvious facts. Do not paraphrase—just use words in the text.

3. What does it mean?
What spiritual lessons or principles can be learned from these facts?

4. Now, what does it mean in my life?
Rewrite the lessons/principles from Step 3 in the form of a personal question.

PART 5

PRINCIPLES FOR LIFE: DEALING WITH STRESS

What, then, do David, Daniel, Elijah, and Joseph have in common? What had each of these men—in their different eras and stations in life—learned about guarding their hearts that can transcend generations and apply to us today?

First, each one learned the secret of submitting their will, their plan, their agenda to God's plan for them. They knew what God had called them to do, yet submitted to His timing.

Second, each of these men had an ambition, each had a choice, each had temptations as a result of that choice (as do we); and each had a level of stress that many of us will never know. From them we can learn a few biblical principles when dealing with stress in our own lives. In fact, these principles apply in other times of difficulty and are not limited just to stress.

A rubber band, if stretched, will return to its normal, relaxed position when the external force is removed. The body's stress response is stretched when faced with any emergency or demand, kind of like a rubber band. When you stop applying external pressure, the rubber band returns to normal unless it is stretched to the point of snapping. We are like a rubber band when exposed to continual stress, and it's difficult to cope with.

What do you do when you're stressed and stretched to the breaking point? I believe David, short and to the point, said it best: "Pour out your hearts to him, for God is our refuge" (Psalm 62:8).

Martha, when stretched to her absolute limit, did exactly this, although she didn't get the response she was expecting:

> *As Jesus and his disciples were on their way, he came to a village where a woman named Martha opened her home to him. She had a sister called Mary, who sat at the Lord's feet listening to what he said. But Martha was distracted by all the preparations that had to be made. She came to him and asked, "Lord, don't you care that my sister has left me to do the work by myself? Tell her to help me!" "Martha, Martha," the Lord answered, "you are worried and upset about many things, but few things are needed—or indeed only one. Mary has chosen what is better, and it will not be taken away from her"* (Luke 10:38-42).

Let's look at some biblical principles for dealing with stress.

Acknowledge It

Stress creates all manner of negative emotions such as anxiety, worry, fear, guilt, shame, and depression. This is what Elijah experienced. It can certainly create frustration. This is the stress David was dealing with when he said, "In my alarm I said, 'I am cut off from your sight!' Yet you heard my cry for mercy when I called to you for help" (Psalm 31:22). He didn't ignore, deny, or pretend his stress was not affecting him. Rather, he acknowledged it was there and was perfectly honest about how it was affecting his emotions and his perspective. Whereas some of us repress our negative emotions, pushing them further and further down, David released his frustrations to God. He wrote, and wrote, and wrote, and his writings are boldly honest.

Part 5: Principles for Life: Dealing with Stress

We sometimes have a hard time being honest about the stress we're under—after all, good, growing Christians don't experience stress (or depression, or conflict for that matter), right? If you find it difficult to acknowledge, maybe seeing it as a weakness in yourself, read through the Psalms and you'll find you're in good company. Not only David but Moses and Solomon write about their times of stress. Also note how they deal with it. Often their hearts are turned to remembering and recounting all the good that God is and does.

It's important to acknowledge when you are under stress. God doesn't want you to suppress your emotions or just tell yourself everything's all right. He understands that stressful circumstances create certain emotions. God created the emotions you're feeling, and He wants you to voice them to Him. Just give Him the unedited version of your frustrations, emotions, and feelings. He's bigger than all of it.

I cannot imagine a more stressful time in the life of any man—ever—than what Jesus lived through one dark night in a garden called Gethsemane. During that night His stress began to build:

> Then Jesus went with his disciples to a place called Gethsemane, and he said to them, "Sit here while I go over there and pray." He took Peter and the two sons of Zebedee along with him, and he began to be sorrowful and troubled. Then he said to them, "My soul is overwhelmed with sorrow to the point of death. Stay here and keep watch with me." Going a little farther, he fell with his face to the ground and prayed, "My Father, if it is possible, may this cup be taken from me. Yet not as I will, but as you will." Then he returned to his disciples and found them sleeping. "Couldn't you men keep watch with me for one hour?" he asked Peter. "Watch and pray so that you will not fall into temptation. The spirit is willing, but the flesh is weak." He

> went away a second time and prayed, "My Father, if it is not possible for this cup to be taken away unless I drink it, may your will be done." When he came back, he again found them sleeping, because their eyes were heavy. So he left them and went away once more and prayed the third time, saying the same thing (Matthew 26:36-44).

Luke describes Jesus's stress this way: "And being in anguish, he prayed more earnestly, and his sweat was like drops of blood falling to the ground. When he rose from prayer and went back to the disciples, he found them asleep, exhausted from sorrow" (Luke 22:44-45).

Jesus understood fully what lay ahead of Him: His arrest, betrayals by more than one of His closest friends, multiple beatings, the brutality. *And He poured out His heart to His Father.* His sweat was like drops of blood falling to the ground, and I suspect that the physical stress wasn't as great as the stress building toward the spiritual battle He knew was ahead of Him. Whatever level of stress you are at, Jesus has been there and *knows* what you are dealing with. Pour out your heart to Him; be as honest with Him as He was with the Father.

I knew a family that lived with an ever-growing stressful situation for over twelve years. Over time they learned, each in their own way, to follow David's example, although not without making a few mistakes along the way. One ignored what was happening but experienced growing anxiety. One stuffed their feelings and began suffering from depression. A third responded to the stress with anger toward others that escalated quickly to rage. When you are exposed to stress that is not dealt with appropriately, over time anxiety, worry, fear, guilt, shame, and depression can become more and more prevalent.

We have a God who gives us complete freedom to say, "Here it is! Here's how I feel, the good, the bad, and the ugly. I'm stressed. I'm frustrated. I'm irritated. I'm angry. I'm depressed."

Part 5: Principles for Life: Dealing with Stress

Whatever you're feeling, the Bible says, "Pour out your heart to God."

But it doesn't stop there. One psalm in which David poured out his heart is Psalm 124. Here we see that he did two specific things that were crucial to coping with the stress he was experiencing. First, a spirit of thankfulness permeates every verse; and second, he acknowledges that his help is in the name of the Lord:

> *If the Lord had not been on our side—let Israel say—if the Lord had not been on our side when people attacked us, they would have swallowed us alive when their anger flared against us; the flood would have engulfed us, the torrent would have swept over us, the raging waters would have swept us away. Praise be to the Lord, who has not let us be torn by their teeth. We have escaped like a bird from the fowler's snare; the snare has been broken, and we have escaped. Our help is in the name of the Lord, the Maker of heaven and earth* (Psalm 124).

There are a number of occasions in David's rather hectic life when he could have written this psalm:

- When he went alone into the valley to face Goliath.
- When Saul eyed him with hate out of jealousy and fear that David was becoming more popular with the people.
- When time and time again he and his men escaped from Saul's army.
- When his son Absalom rebelled and tried to kill him.
- During one of his wars with Syria and Edom.

David found it virtually impossible to remain fixed on his circumstances and fears because his eyes were fixed on God. You know, God isn't up there devising ways to put us in our place, to knock us back, to teach us a lesson. It says here plainly, "God has not given us over to be torn apart." That is not what He does.

One of the values of God's Word is that it puts into words for us those deep feelings of our hearts we would have trouble expressing any other way. Who hasn't felt some of these things: attacked, raged against, a torrent sweeping over you, being trapped? What is it that has you feeling trapped and cornered? Can God make a way for you? Psalm 124 is where we need to go when we're hemmed in on every side and everything looks hopeless, when we are up against insurmountable odds and the stress is mounting. This type of psalm is key in guarding the heart because it prompts us to give thanks with a gratefulness God deserves. It realigns our focus from our circumstances and onto the power of His name. Read the book of Acts if you need to be reminded of this power!

Receive Help from Others

There is the temptation when we're stressed out and at the breaking point to isolate ourselves. We want to say, "I don't want anybody around me right now. I'm too stressed to deal with anyone." That's a mistake. When we are at our breaking point and stressed to the limit, we need people in our life. Ask for God's wisdom who to let in to help you (because let's face it, sometimes people do or say the worst things with the best motives). We need people who will give us support, give us strength, and most of all give us perspective. When we're stressed, we don't think straight, we don't see clearly, and our perspective is limited. We need somebody else who can help us see the bigger picture. We need people around when we're at the breaking point.

But we need those kinds of relationships in place before the crisis! When the storms come into our life and those hurricane winds sweep in is not the time to find friends or to get into a small group.[18]

"Encourage each other and give each other strength" (1 Thessalonians 5:11 NCV). Remember from Part 1 when David was in the cave and Jonathan came and "encouraged him in the Lord"? In that desolate mountain cave God showed David He was still there by doing two things: First, He made David aware that his life was in danger. Second, miles away, God moved Jonathan to go and seek out his friend David. Sometimes we get so messed up, confused, and overwhelmed, that we need someone to make Him real again. With Jonathan's help, David began to remember what he knew to be true about God, and his faith grew on that.

Never underestimate the power of just a little word of encouragement. You may need to make a phone call this afternoon, or send a text, or write someone a note. It doesn't have to be long—just a note to show you care, a note of encouragement. My husband has a file called "Good Things," and in it are many of the notes and cards people have written him over the years. When he's discouraged, he knows they're there and draws encouragement from that—although he may not actually get them out and read them.

We all need to receive help from others because by helping each other with our troubles, we obey the law of Christ (Galatians 6:2).

Focus on Christ

The Apostle Paul talks about some of his own stressful experiences:

I have worked much harder, been in prison

more frequently, been flogged more severely, and been exposed to death again and again. Five times I received from the Jews the forty lashes minus one. Three times I was beaten with rods, once I was pelted with stones, three times I was shipwrecked, I spent a night and a day in the open sea, I have been constantly on the move. I have been in danger from rivers, in danger from bandits, in danger from my fellow Jews, in danger from Gentiles; in danger in the city, in danger in the country, in danger at sea; and in danger from false believers. I have labored and toiled and have often gone without sleep; I have known hunger and thirst and have often gone without food; I have been cold and naked. Besides everything else, I face daily the pressure of my concern for all the churches (2 Corinthians 11:23-28).

That's his experience. Now see Paul's perspective:

Therefore, since through God's mercy we have this ministry, we do not lose heart.... For God, who said, "Let light shine out of darkness," made his light shine in our hearts to give us the light of the knowledge of God's glory displayed in the face of Christ. But we have this treasure in jars of clay to show that this all-surpassing power is from God and not from us. We are hard pressed on every side, but not crushed; perplexed, but not in despair; persecuted, but not abandoned; struck down, but not destroyed.... Therefore we do not lose heart. Though outwardly we are wasting away, yet inwardly we are being renewed day by day. For our light and momentary troubles are achieving for us an eternal glory that far outweighs them all. So we fix our eyes not on what is seen, but on what is unseen, since what is seen is temporary, but what is unseen is eternal (2 Corinthians 4:1, 6-9, 16-18).

Perspective is crucial. For example, you may have been bitten by a dog as a child with the resulting conviction that all dogs are terrorizing. Your perception is causing an emotional response, which may be totally irrational, but valid nonetheless because it is not just things that are happening to you, or the situation you find yourself in, it is your *perception* of what is happening (or has happened) to you.

Gaining a kingdom perspective is essential. As one friend said, "If you don't like something, change it; if you can't change it, change the way you think about it." This is important because when we're under stress, our life gets out of focus. In fact, when we're under stress we start looking at our problem and stop looking at Christ. We need to allow God to come in at the perception level and provide us with His perspective. He wants us to walk in *His* light, not our own. Your perception will impact how you pray.

Remember Elijah in his mountain cave, rattling off his list of injustices? His perspective was all wrong, and it affected not only his physical state but his spiritual state as well.

Verse 8 of Psalm 124 says: "Our help is in the name of the Lord, the Maker of heaven and earth." The early disciples understood the power in the name of Jesus, and they knew how to use that power to receive His blessings and bless others.

Today, many Christians don't realize the power that is behind the name of Jesus—but Satan *does*. He hates Jesus and wants to desensitize the world to His name. In fact, the Bible is filled with testimony after testimony to the power of the name of Jesus. Here are just a few:

- "Everyone who calls on the name of the Lord will be saved. Salvation is found in no one else, for there is no other name under heaven given to mankind by which

- we must be saved" (Romans 10:13; Acts 4:12).
- "Then Peter said, 'Silver or gold I do not have, but what I do have I give you. In the name of Jesus Christ of Nazareth, walk'" (Acts 3:6).
- "By faith in the name of Jesus, this man whom you see and know was made strong. It is Jesus' name and the faith that comes through him that has completely healed him, as you can all see" (Acts 3:16).
- "Once when we were going to the place of prayer, we were met by a female slave who had a spirit by which she predicted the future. She earned a great deal of money for her owners by fortune-telling. She followed Paul and the rest of us, shouting, 'These men are servants of the Most High God, who are telling you the way to be saved.' She kept this up for many days. Finally Paul became so annoyed that he turned around and said to the spirit, 'In the name of Jesus Christ I command you to come out of her!' At that moment the spirit left her. When her owners realized that their hope of making money was gone, they seized Paul and Silas and dragged them into the marketplace to face the authorities" (Acts 16:16-18).
- "Therefore God exalted him to the highest place and gave him the name that is above every name, that at the name of Jesus every knee should bow, in heaven and on earth and under the earth, and every tongue acknowledge that Jesus Christ is Lord, to the glory of God the Father" (Philippians 2:9-11).

Don't Let Bitterness Take Root

There is a pattern emerging here, and if you were to go through the lives of David, Daniel, Elijah, and Joseph (and Paul) you would note their resistance to becoming bitter. Okay, Elijah had a bit of a go at it in his cave experience (Part 3), but once he faced God with his issues, they were dealt with and

Part 5: Principles for Life: Dealing with Stress

they were not able to take root.

The Bible tells us that bitterness is far more devastating to your life than stress is, which is what Joseph learned (we touched on this briefly in Part 4). He had a lot to be bitter about, and not only could he have been justifiably bitter toward his family, in the early days bitterness toward God would not have been out of the question. And, during his prison years, he would have had a lot of time on his hands to dwell on the injustices in his life, and the fact that the perpetrators—from his brothers to his masters—were going unchallenged and unpunished.

In the long run, bitterness will hurt you more than the actual circumstances that you're going through. It is like blood poisoning—sepsis—which permeates every part of your body, affecting vital organs, and eventually leading to death. Sepsis is a potentially deadly medical condition characterized by a whole-body inflammatory state. That pretty much describes bitterness!

The Bible is very clear about the danger of allowing bitterness to reside in your heart: "See to it that no one falls short of the grace of God and that no bitter root grows up to cause trouble and defile many" (Hebrews 12:15). What is in your heart shows on your face; anger glares from the eyes, disapproval pulls the mouth down—it's ugly, and that's just the start.

Bitterness does not affect just you, but others around you bear the brunt of it. Relationships are broken. Harsh words once said can't be taken back and are seldom forgotten by the one on the receiving end of them. I once worked with someone who was so unpleasant that my stomach would begin churning the closer to work I got each morning. My aunt used to call her neighbor "old misery guts." Is that how we want to be known?

Is there another choice besides bitterness? Yes. Thankfulness is the antidote to bitterness. Studies have shown that thankfulness and gratitude are the healthiest emotions you can possibly have. Although gratitude and thankfulness are often used interchangeably, gratitude is actually the quality of being thankful. We're told to "give thanks with a *grateful* heart." To be thankful is more of an outward expression of appreciating something. I can be thankful for a lot of things, but being grateful brings my emotions into my thankfulness.

In fact, did you know that it is actually a sin to be *unthankful*, and one that carries consequences? "For although they knew God, they neither glorified him as God nor gave thanks to him, but their thinking became futile and their foolish hearts were darkened" (Romans 1:21). You cannot be thankful and bitter at the same time. I came across the following story which illustrates this point and puts the right perspective on thankfulness.

While Chen Min Lin pastored three house-churches in China, he was arrested for preaching the gospel. He had been arrested two times prior, but this time, he was imprisoned in despicable Chinese prisons for eighteen years. His wife died and his young son was killed while he suffered in unspeakable conditions, but his communist captors withheld this information from Pastor Chen.

Pastor Chen wasn't the only one to suffer horrid prison conditions. The communist government took the growing Christian population as a threat to their power; therefore, they put all Christian ministers in prison.

Watching his Christian brothers die one by one in torture chambers, Pastor Chen also longed to die at times. Years passed slowly in the Chinese prison and the prison guards assigned Pastor Chen to work in the prison camp's cesspool—a death sentence in those days. He used rosin and coated his socks, making them resistant to the infectious water. And he prayed for God's protection.

Pastor Chen thought for sure he would die that first day—the smell was sickening. The foul job and stench was just as sickening to the prison guards.

The second morning working in the cesspool, he noticed something—he was completely alone. A rare occurrence in a crowded prison camp.

As the blessing of solitude washed over him, he began to

softly sing. Something he hadn't been able to do since being thrown into prison years before. He worshiped and sang louder. As tears ran down his face, he sang an old hymn he learned as a young convert. That song took on a personal meaning for him.

After each verse and chorus, he seemed to smell the fragrant aroma of the Rose of Sharon—even in a stinking cesspool. The Holy Spirit transformed that dark place into a beautiful garden of life and light.[19]

What Pastor Chen Min Lin learned was the art of giving thanks with a grateful heart through having his perspective transformed by the power of the Holy Spirit. Although his circumstances had not changed, his heart had.

Shortly after I became a believer (two weeks actually), I went to a one-year Bible school in Southern California. For the previous seven years my life had been centered around drugs and alcohol, and when an opportunity was offered to me to escape the pulls of that lifestyle, I was only too happy to take it.

When I arrived at the school, one of the first people I met was Joy. We actually had an extraordinary amount of similarities: We were both the third daughter out of four children (with the long-awaited son being the fourth). We both had fathers who were preachers. We were scrutinized and judged in a way only preachers' kids are. We were expected to behave like good Christians, make the right choices, and be nice. However, when I was introduced to Joy I remember my very first thought was, "*I don't like you.*" She had done nothing to me or against me, but I took an immediate and unreasonable dislike to her.

I knew instinctively why I didn't like her—she was everything that I should have been, and wanted to be, but was not. I resented the fact that she had made the right choices where I had made wrong ones. She had never smoked; I smoked three packs a day—you get the picture. Jealousy led to resentfulness, which was fast becoming bitterness every time someone said something nice about her.

However, as soon as those "I don't like you" words formed in my mind, I was aware of God's presence, and His unexpectedly quiet voice saying to my heart, "Don't you go down that road. I want you to thank Me for Joy every day." And do you know what? I couldn't do it. I *wanted* to, but the words stuck. The best I could do, from September until Christmas, was to croak out the word *thank*. By Easter I got as far as *thank you*. It was a long road, but I desperately wanted to please God, to have my hardened heart transformed, and I knew that obedience was the only way to do it.

By the time the year ended, I was able to say, "Thank you for Joy." Not only with truthfulness, but with a gratefulness that God loved me so much He was going to instruct me Himself as to how to guard my heart; how to thank Him for what I didn't want to thank Him for. (Incidentally she ended up becoming a very dear friend, a relationship I would have missed out on completely had I indulged my unreasonable perspective of her.) What I learned was the art of giving thanks with a grateful heart through having my perspective transformed by the power of the Holy Spirit, and although my circumstances had not changed—I still had "a past"—my heart had changed and bitterness didn't take root.

Bitterness is often a by-product of finding ourselves stressed to the breaking point. We start feeling bitter and resentful and are convinced that "This shouldn't be happening to me." The fact is, we're going to be hurt in life—by circumstances, by things, by other people, sometimes intentionally and sometimes unintentionally, but we're going to be hurt. We can't keep ourselves from being hurt. While we may not control what happens to us, we *can* control how we choose to react to a particular circumstance or person who has hurt us.

Paul says in 1 Thessalonians 5:18, "Give thanks in all circumstances; for this is God's will for you in Christ Jesus." Reading this verse, it made me think of the story of Corrie ten Boom. Corrie ten Boom lived in Holland with her family, and during WWII they were Christians who hid Jewish people in their home to keep them from being captured by the Nazis.

They had a little attic where they hid them, and it was called the hiding place.

Corrie and her family were caught and sent to a concentration camp called Ravensbruck. Corrie and her sister started a Bible study in their barracks. One day they talked about the verse, "In everything give thanks, for this is God's will" and wondered what they could be thankful for in the middle of a holocaust? They decided to be thankful for the fleas. Their barracks were infested with fleas. After a couple of days, they realized that the fleas kept the German guards from entering their barracks; therefore, they weren't abused by the guards and could have as many Bible studies as they wanted. They thanked God for the fleas.[20]

Even in the most hopeless of situations, you can find something to thank God for. This is what Joseph learned. If anyone had a "right" to bitterness, I think he would qualify. Captivity was where he learned to have a grateful heart rather than feed a bitter soul, finding a way to live with the consequences of another's sin, without it becoming a bondage of bitterness.

Refocus on God and His Promises

Daniel was a God-centered man with a God-centered view of his world who challenged this world with his personal view of God; yet he, too, would have had his moments of discouragement and disappointment from the stress of a life spent in exile.

He somehow had to come to terms with the fact that he was now living with the consequences of the sins of his parents' and grandparents' generation. *They* weren't the ones in exile, *he* was. In Daniel chapter nine he was reading the book of Jeremiah, and I wonder if he was trying to get God's perspective on the whole mess. As he studied the prophecies of Jeremiah, he was experiencing the destruction and exile firsthand, yet there was absolutely no doubt in his mind but that God was at the center of it all, and it turned his heart to Him (Daniel 9:3). Daniel was able to stay God-centered, rather than blame God, because he was fully focused on God's promises found in His Word, and in his prayer here, he repeatedly refers to what God has promised to do.

Daniel acknowledges God as "the great and awesome God"; He is a God who "keeps his covenant and mercy" shows "mercy and forgiveness"; He confirms His word in holy judgment; His word is truth; He is a deliverer of the oppressed.

Learn to ask God for His perspective. He loves to answer this type of prayer! Paul sums it up better than anyone in Philippians 4:4-6:

- *Rejoice in the Lord always* (even in the stress, anxiety and despair of your life).
- *Let your gentleness be evident to all* (don't become bitter; *gentle* means "a non-fighting spirit").
- *The Lord is near* (He is aware of your struggles, wanting to be drawn in to help).
- *Do not be anxious about anything, but in every situation, by prayer and petition, with thanksgiving, present your requests to God* (refocus, refocus, refocus).
- *And the peace of God, which transcends all understanding, will guard your hearts and your minds in Christ Jesus* (a peace that is far more healing than any amount of resentfulness or bitterness).

Recognize and acknowledge your stress. Receive help from others whom God brings into your life. Refuse to let bitterness take root. Refocus on God and His promises. These are the key elements we see in the lives of David, Daniel, Elijah, and Joseph.

PART 5: PRINCIPLES FOR LIFE: DEALING WITH STRESS

Dealing with Stress

1. **Read Psalm 31.**
   Underline, circle, or mark the text that speaks to you.

In you, Lord, I have taken refuge;
   let me never be put to shame;
   deliver me in your righteousness.
² Turn your ear to me,
   come quickly to my rescue;
be my rock of refuge,
   a strong fortress to save me.
³ Since you are my rock and my fortress,
   for the sake of your name lead and guide me.
⁴ Keep me free from the trap that is set for me,
   for you are my refuge.
⁵ Into your hands I commit my spirit;
   deliver me, Lord, my faithful God.

⁶ I hate those who cling to worthless idols;
   as for me, I trust in the Lord.
⁷ I will be glad and rejoice in your love,
   for you saw my affliction
   and knew the anguish of my soul.
⁸ You have not given me into the hands of the enemy
   but have set my feet in a spacious place.

⁹ Be merciful to me, Lord, for I am in distress;
   my eyes grow weak with sorrow,
   my soul and body with grief.
¹⁰ My life is consumed by anguish
   and my years by groaning;
my strength fails because of my affliction,
   and my bones grow weak.
¹¹ Because of all my enemies,
   I am the utter contempt of my neighbors
and an object of dread to my closest friends—
   those who see me on the street flee from me.
¹² I am forgotten as though I were dead;

I have become like broken pottery.
¹³ For I hear many whispering,
   "Terror on every side!"
They conspire against me
   and plot to take my life.

¹⁴ But I trust in you, Lord;
   I say, "You are my God."
¹⁵ My times are in your hands;
   deliver me from the hands of my enemies,
   from those who pursue me.
¹⁶ Let your face shine on your servant;
   save me in your unfailing love.
¹⁷ Let me not be put to shame, Lord,
   for I have cried out to you;
but let the wicked be put to shame
   and be silent in the realm of the dead.
¹⁸ Let their lying lips be silenced,
   for with pride and contempt
   they speak arrogantly against the righteous.

¹⁹ How abundant are the good things
   that you have stored up for those who fear you,
that you bestow in the sight of all,
   on those who take refuge in you.
²⁰ In the shelter of your presence you hide them
   from all human intrigues;
you keep them safe in your dwelling
   from accusing tongues.

²¹ Praise be to the Lord,
   for he showed me the wonders of his love
   when I was in a city under siege.
²² In my alarm I said,
   "I am cut off from your sight!"
Yet you heard my cry for mercy
   when I called to you for help.

²³ Love the Lord, all his faithful people!
   The Lord preserves those who are true to him,
   but the proud he pays back in full.

PART 5: PRINCIPLES FOR LIFE: DEALING WITH STRESS

²⁴ Be strong and take heart,
   all you who hope in the Lord.

2. What does it say?
Make a verse-by-verse list of the most outstanding, obvious facts. Do not paraphrase—just use words in the text.

3. What does it mean?
What spiritual lessons or principles can be learned from these facts?

4. Now, what does it mean in my life?
Rewrite the lessons/principles from Step 3 in the form of a personal question.

PART 6

PRINCIPLES FOR LIFE: SUBMISSION

One other factor that David, Daniel, Elijah, and Joseph had in common—something critical to their deep personal relationship with God—is that each one *submitted their will to God's will*. Submission is not a word that men or women respond to well, or with much enthusiasm. This word has been misunderstood, misused, and misapplied for centuries. It has come to mean being under the power of someone else in a negative way, having to accept the authority or control of someone else, who may or may not handle their authority appropriately.

Submission simply means giving up our need to control. Our need to control decisions at work; our need to control all the decisions in our home; our need to control everything and everyone.

The idea of submission is interwoven with the fact that David sought God's will in everything. The idea of submission is integral to Daniel turning away from embracing what the world would have him do. It is why Elijah went back to Jezreel and went from spiritual strength to strength until he was taken by God to heaven in a whirlwind. Submission is what enabled Joseph to stop asking "Why?" and begin to ask "For what purpose?"

We have seen how powerful it was for God's kingdom when these men submitted their plans and ambitions to God's will for them, as difficult and complicated as it seemed to make their lives. Satan also knows how powerful submission is, which is exactly why he does *not* want us to live this way. So he has come up with untruths about submission (both submission to God and to each other) that we often end up believing at some level.

Let's look at four false beliefs we have about submission.

Submitting to God Means I Lose My Freedom

Contrary to popular belief, submission isn't just a woman's lot in life—it is the *believer's* lot in life. And you have two choices: You can submit in obedience, or you can grasp what you feel is yours by right.

For example, David was God's anointed, the kingship was his, and more than once King Saul had been within killing distance (1 Samuel 24:1-5; 26:11-16). David could easily have grasped at what was rightfully his; he was free to do anything he liked. He was the acknowledged leader of a thousand men who were either in distress or in debt or discontented for some reason, and who had nothing to lose. Removing Saul would not have been a problem.

However, David chose a different response—he submitted to God's timing and refused to be swayed from his decision to follow His course. It meant a lot more years in the desert, but the closeness of his relationship with his God was worth more to him than anything else.

For me personally, this imagined "loss of freedom" if I became a Christian was a big sticking point in committing my life to Christ. As trivial as it sounds now, I didn't want to quit smoking. (Which, incidentally, is not a requirement to being a follower of Jesus. Smoking was a taboo incorporated into the belief system of the denomination I grew up in.) I didn't want to lose my friends. I didn't understand that both were killing me. I was totally bound in my "freedom," getting further into debt, further into the drug culture, and more and more desperate.

So much for freedom! I was blind to the fact that I was actually in bondage to sin, and the consequences of it.

The truth is, Jesus said, "I have come that they [we] may have life, and have it to the full" (John 10:10). This is what David understood—that giving up his freedom to live his life God's way without taking matters into his own hands, resulted in a fuller, richer, more blessed life.

Submitting to God Means I Lose My Identity

Our identity is who we are, it's what makes each of us unique; lose that, and we lose ourselves—or so we think. When our identity is tied into what we think we are, we will be more likely to resist submitting to anyone else. We think, "What about *me*? I don't want to lose who *I* am."

During my daughters' school years, I was simply "Christina and Karin's mom." I am often introduced as "Brian's wife," which really annoys one of my friends, who tells me I need to assert myself and insist that I have a name. What I try to explain is that these relationships are a part of me; I am happy to be "Jean Phillips's daughter," or "the lady married to the Canadian guy." I don't lose myself to these people. They don't *define* me (I know exactly who I am), rather I am enhanced by my relationship with them, and I don't mind people knowing it.

People often confuse Elijah with Elisha: "Which one was it that did that miracle?" Talk about loss of personal identity! But I suspect neither one of these men would have minded being confused with the other, but rather would have taken it as a compliment.

I remember reading about a motivational speaker, Zig Ziglar, and the way he liked to introduce himself. He would say, "Hi, I am Mrs. Ziglar's happy husband!" Why say that? Love. Love delights in assuming the identity of the one loved, in marriage, in friendship, even in work.[21] I keep trying to get Brian to introduce himself as "Mrs. Jose's happy husband" with no success...yet.

Submission is no problem where there is love. When Jesus submitted to His Father, He didn't lose His identity—He knew exactly who He was: the Anointed One, the Messiah. His identity wasn't lost, it was *enhanced* because of His relationship of submission to His Father, whom He loved more than life itself:

> *During the days of Jesus' life on earth, he offered up prayers and petitions with fervent cries and tears to the one who could save him from death, and he was heard because of his reverent submission. Son though he was, he learned obedience from what he suffered and, once made perfect, he became the source of eternal salvation for all who obey him* (Hebrews 5:7-9).

Submitting to God Means I Lose Control

We think we will no longer be able to decide for ourselves what we should and shouldn't do—which person to marry; what career path to follow. We are raised to be "independent." Submitting what *we* want to what *God* wants goes against everything we were taught.

Before I became a believer, my world was so narrow, I was casting about not knowing what to do with my life, and making unwise choices. Since submitting my will, what *I* want (and not even knowing half the time what that even was!), my life has taken many unexpected turns but always with a purpose: to "remove the stones from the highway of God's people" (Isaiah 62:10). This verse was given to me when I was being asked to move from a place I loved to a place I didn't know because God had prepared and was moving my husband in that direction.

I could have pressed to stay where we were, there were many good reasons to. But in that act of submission, my own ministry was developed, encouraged, and given life. I thought I would lose speaking opportunities, but they have actually increased. I thought I would never be able to "remove stones" in the lives of God's people in Albania because of the language barrier, but the truth is God has brought into my life women who are living through what I have personally experienced over the course of my life and who need the encouragement I can offer because I understand exactly what they're dealing with. What a richness I would have lost if I had refused to submit to where God was leading me (through my husband!). We don't always see God's purpose initially, and this is where faith comes in. Faith that God isn't going to lead us into something that is demeaning, or in any way detrimental to our spiritual growth.

During the years that Brian and I transported Bibles into Eastern Europe, we also took in other Christian literature. One group wrote their material, had it printed on their premises, and our group smuggled it into the country and into the hands of the pastors it was destined for. Then this first group sent people in a few weeks later to teach, discuss, and help these pastors learn to search Scripture and apply it. I didn't travel as much as Brian did, so two days a week I worked in the office of this group, taking an absolute mess of handwritten notes and typing them into a readable format ready for printing.

However, when I arrived on my first day to do this really worthwhile ministry, the stench of the place almost knocked me over—six men had been working in this house for months with only one toilet, and none of them seemed to have had a sense of smell or basic hygiene, because it was appalling. So I cleaned it. The next week it was in a bad state again, so I cleaned it. It's the story of my life: Audrey Jose; Female; Created in God's image to do great things for His kingdom; Cleaner of toilets. I had every right to say, "Hey, I wasn't hired for this! Who do you people think you are expecting the woman to do the cleaning? How dare you demean me this way! I'm not going to do this—I have better things to do!"

I could easily have grasped at what I believed was rightfully mine—a position of responsibility that I was volunteering for. But you know what? Twenty-one years later, Brian saw the director of this organization at a conference, and after the initial "man hugs" and catching up, he said to Brian, "Your wife made an impression on me that I've never forgotten. She taught me to clean a toilet."

The point of this story isn't to make me look good but to illustrate that it is possible to submit, in obedience, to Jesus's example. And by doing so, to live out, through your actions, a principle that can leave a lasting impression for the good in someone else's life.

Grasping never achieves this. Submitting—letting go of the need to control—does. It may feel like it will kill us to submit to someone else, especially someone we do not have much respect for, if they have an authority we feel they don't deserve or are abusing their role. The secret lies in Jesus's example, because He's not asking us to do anything He hasn't lived through Himself: "When they hurled their insults at him, he did not retaliate; when he suffered, he made no threats. Instead, he entrusted himself to him who judges justly" (1 Peter 2:23). He entrusted Himself to Him who judges justly.

There Is No Joy in Submitting to God

Joy. What is it, anyway? What does it mean? It certainly means more than simply *happiness*. I posted this question on Facebook and my friend Pam commented that joy is to know the love of God and passing it on to others. Knowing, accepting, and experiencing God's love.

What we seldom realize when we buy into the lie that there is no joy if we submit to God is when we submit to God, we can trust Him to see our pain, know our hurt, and work things out for our good and His glory. And yes, actually bring joy into our life. This may take some time, and again, this is where faith comes in—faith that God will do what He says He will do. And we need to submit for Him and not for anyone else.

Jesus didn't consider submission a loss of joy. He looked at the cross and decided that submission would be a joy: "For the joy set before him he endured the cross, scorning its shame, and sat down at the right hand of the throne of God" (Hebrews 12:2). I believe we buy into this lie because we don't really understand what submission is. We often think it is being told what to do (and not wanting to do it), being bossed around, not ever getting our own way.

In Philippians chapter 2, Paul says:

> *In your relationships with one another, have the same mindset as Christ Jesus: Who, being in very nature God, did not consider equality with God something to be used to his own advantage; rather, he made himself nothing by taking the very nature of a servant, being made in human likeness. And being found in appearance as a man, he humbled himself by becoming obedient to death—even death on a cross! Therefore God exalted him to the highest place and gave him the name that is above every name, that at the name of Jesus every knee should bow, in heaven and on earth and under the earth, and every tongue acknowledge that Jesus Christ is Lord, to the glory of God the Father* (Philippians 2:5-11).

He humbled Himself, which means that by becoming a servant, He thought of us more than He thought of Himself. Why? Out of obedience. For no other reason. He knew who He was. He chose to submit; He submitted in obedience.

Obedience vs. Submission

It's quite possible to obey without submitting. Obedience is an outward action, while submission is an inward attitude. God calls us to more than just blind obedience.

A mother told her disobedient son to sit in a corner. After

a couple of minutes of sitting, he told her, "I'm sitting down on the outside, but I'm standing up on the inside!" He obeyed, but he didn't submit.[22] It is just as much an attitude of the heart issue as it is an action issue.

The word *obedient* used to describe Jesus's attitude in the above passage in Philippians 2 is the word *hupekoos* and means "attentively listening, by implication submissive" and is a derivative of the word *hupakouo*, which means "to hear under (as a subordinate), that is, to listen attentively; by implication to heed or conform to a command or authority" and is translated: "hearken, be obedient to, obey."[23]

Basically this means to pay close attention to someone's needs. It is the idea of attending to the needs of another. It doesn't mean doing everything they want, the instant they want it. However, Satan wants you to believe that if you start being responsive in this obedient way, you will be walked all over—it will just encourage others to order you around. That is not true.

How did David submit? He practiced the presence of God in his life by calling on the name of God for direction. He chose to live a life of purity, no matter what people thought; for example, letting Saul live when he didn't have to. He persevered and saw God's power in his powerlessness in the caves, in the deserts. He made choices based on his knowledge of a God who was personal to him. His heart of prayer was poured out in what are now our Psalms.

How did Daniel submit? He practiced the presence of God in his life through daily prayer. He chose to live a life of purity, no matter what the cost. He persevered and saw God's power in his weakness when various kings made sweeping decrees that landed him in a lions' den. He prayed and everyone knew it.

How did Elijah submit? He practiced the presence of God in his life by obediently going where God directed him. His motives were pure in God's eyes, no matter what King Ahab or Queen Jezebel taunted him with. He persevered and saw God's power in his weakness on the remote cliff of a barren mountain. He prayed and God answered in mighty, powerful ways.

How did Joseph submit? He practiced the presence of

Part 6: Principles for Life: Submission

God in his life by acknowledging God's control. He was able to maintain a life of purity, even through humiliation, being lied about, and prison. He persevered and witnessed God's power made strong through his weakness day after long, lonely day. He made choices, and the underpinning of each choice was prayerfully seeking God's perspective as to how and where God had shown grace to him, and opening himself up to God's greater plan—a much better plan than revenge.

There are many instances in the Bible where God asked people to submit for a bigger purpose. We've already talked about Hagar who gave up on life because her mistress treated her so poorly. But God in heaven, the creator of the universe, looked down and saw one woman, alone and crying, and He came down and spoke to her.

Hagar had stopped near a well, and after her talk with God, she named it "The well of the One who lives and sees me." Our God is this same God—the one who lives and sees you and me. He is a personal God, concerned about abused women and unborn babies. And He wants us to see Him and respond to Him in submission and obedience as Hagar did...because God told her to do something very hard: "Go back to the one you are running away from and trust me" (Genesis 16:9).

God told Hagar to submit to Sarah so she would see God's grace at work: "But where sin increased, grace increased all the more" (Romans 5:20). This means God's grace was greater than Sarah's sinful behavior and attitude. God wanted Hagar to understand that His grace can accomplish His best even when others do their worst.

Hagar did return and submit herself to Sarah. She did trust God to protect her and her son and to care for them in the years to come. In fact her son, Ishmael, grew to be the father of a great nation because God keeps His promises and He had promised her: "I will increase your descendants so much that they will be too numerous to count." The angel of the Lord also said to her: "You are now pregnant and you will give birth to a son. You shall name him Ishmael, for the Lord has heard of your misery" (Genesis 16:10-11).

We never solve life's problems by running away. But when we submit to God, we *can* trust Him to see our pain, know our hurt, and to work things out for our good and His glory. But that may take a long time, and that is where faith comes in—faith in a God who keeps His promises.[24]

Jonah is another example in the Bible of submitting to God for a bigger purpose; however, he learned the lesson of submission and obedience the hard way. In fact, I'm not sure he ever really learned the lesson at all—he was one of those sitting in the corner on the outside but standing up on the inside! God told him to go to a specific place and preach a message of repentance and salvation, and he did the exact opposite. He thumbed his nose at God and said, "I understand very well what You want me to do, but I don't agree with You. So, I'm going to go my own way, do my own thing." God said go east, and he boarded a ship going the opposite direction. However, after a rather traumatic three days in a fish's stomach (the consequence of his own decisions and choices), he did eventually submit and obey:

> God in heaven, the creator of the universe, looked down and saw one woman, alone and crying, and He came down and spoke to her.

> *Jonah obeyed the word of the Lord and went to Nineveh. Now Nineveh was a very large city; it took three days to go through it. Jonah began by going a day's journey into the city, proclaiming, "Forty more days and Nineveh will be overthrown." The Ninevites believed God. A fast was proclaimed, and all of them, from the greatest to the least, put on sackcloth. When Jonah's warning reached the king of*

> Nineveh, he rose from his throne, took off his royal robes, covered himself with sackcloth and sat down in the dust. This is the proclamation he issued in Nineveh: "By the decree of the king and his nobles: Do not let people or animals, herds or flocks, taste anything; do not let them eat or drink. But let people and animals be covered with sackcloth. Let everyone call urgently on God. Let them give up their evil ways and their violence. Who knows? God may yet relent and with compassion turn from his fierce anger so that we will not perish." When God saw what they did and how they turned from their evil ways, he relented and did not bring on them the destruction he had threatened (Jonah 3:3-10).

The point here is that time after time, when we look at the lives of men and women in the Bible, we see that submission and obedience have a ripple effect into the lives of others, not just those doing the submitting. Sometimes we need to ask Him to show us because when we're in the middle of an overwhelming situation, we aren't always aware of it. Once again, we need to develop a kingdom perspective, God's perspective, and not simply focus on our own lives and circumstances.

Submission

1. Read Psalm 66.
Underline, circle, or mark the text that speaks to you.

Shout for joy to God, all the earth!
²   Sing the glory of his name;
    make his praise glorious.
³ Say to God, "How awesome are your deeds!
    So great is your power
    that your enemies cringe before you.
⁴ All the earth bows down to you;
    they sing praise to you,
    they sing the praises of your name."

⁵ Come and see what God has done,
    his awesome deeds for mankind!
⁶ He turned the sea into dry land,
    they passed through the waters on foot—
    come, let us rejoice in him.
⁷ He rules forever by his power,
    his eyes watch the nations—
    let not the rebellious rise up against him.

⁸ Praise our God, all peoples,
    let the sound of his praise be heard;
⁹ he has preserved our lives
    and kept our feet from slipping.
¹⁰ For you, God, tested us;
    you refined us like silver.
¹¹ You brought us into prison
    and laid burdens on our backs.
¹² You let people ride over our heads;
    we went through fire and water,
    but you brought us to a place of abundance.

¹³ I will come to your temple with burnt offerings
    and fulfill my vows to you—
¹⁴ vows my lips promised and my mouth spoke
    when I was in trouble.

Part 6: Principles for Life: Submission

¹⁵ I will sacrifice fat animals to you
   and an offering of rams;
   I will offer bulls and goats.

¹⁶ Come and hear, all you who fear God;
   let me tell you what he has done for me.
¹⁷ I cried out to him with my mouth;
   his praise was on my tongue.
¹⁸ If I had cherished sin in my heart,
   the Lord would not have listened;
¹⁹ but God has surely listened
   and has heard my prayer.
²⁰ Praise be to God,
   who has not rejected my prayer
   or withheld his love from me!

2. What does it say?
Make a verse-by-verse list of the most outstanding, obvious facts. Do not paraphrase—just use words in the text.

3. What does it mean?

What spiritual lessons or principles can be learned from these facts?

4. Now, what does it mean in my life?
Rewrite the lessons/principles from Step 3 in the form of a personal question.

CONCLUSION

CONCLUSION

PRINCIPLES FOR LIFE: LEGACY

The Holy Spirit graciously shows us where we need to submit and stop grasping. The Holy Spirit helps us see ourselves as equally created to serve in God's plan, taking spiritual responsibility, becoming a working part of God's kingdom ministry, and leaving a legacy equal to that of:

- David: whose legacy was a nation of worshippers of the One True God. The Psalms he wrote speak straight to our souls, all these thousands of years later, take us straight to the throne of God with the cries of our heart, and lead us into worship. They invite us to practice the presence of God just as David developed the habit of welcoming the presence of God in his life. As a teenager he started with a promise from God that didn't seem at the time to be getting him anywhere. He ended being called "a man after God's own heart."
- Daniel: whose legacy of influence on the authority over him (because of his incorruptibility) brought Nebuchadnezzar into a relationship with God (Daniel 4:34-37). Daniel's integrity made him a valued, trusted lawmaker and counselor to world leaders, whose decisions and laws were far-reaching. He made a stand and lived his life with an unshakeable determination to

remain pure and holy in God's eyes. He ended with a reputation untainted, unimpeachable, and unashamed of his God. His model of living a life of purity inspires us even today to imitate his example.

- Elijah: whose legacy of persevering in the power of the Holy Spirit made him a trustworthy mentor whom God used in a powerful way. Because Elijah persevered with faithful obedience, he ended in the place where God wanted him, humbling himself as Christ did, with a reputation as God's spokesman for the nation. Elisha carried Elijah's legacy—learning from him—and went on in the power of the Holy Spirit to do even greater things than Elijah.

- Joseph: whose legacy of self-sacrifice resulted in the salvation of his family through the freedom forgiveness brought. His steadfast life of prayer reveals to us the power of prayer. He started life not quite knowing how to handle his God-given gifts. He ended by living a life that mirrored Jesus.

> Guarding your heart will leave a legacy.

My prayer for you is that you put into practice the principles of Proverbs 4 and experience for yourself the power that comes from the Holy Spirit once you are truly submitted to the Lord Jesus Christ.

Practicing the presence of God in every area of your life, not picking and choosing; striving to live a life of purity in a world where this is challenged on a daily basis; persevering in seeking His will at all times and through all circumstances—hurricanes, earthquakes and fire— and through prayer seeking God's perspective in areas where you're resentful, bitter, and needing His power to forgive. Guarding your heart in this will leave a legacy that will speak as powerfully in someone else's life as David, Daniel, Elijah, and Joseph's lives speak to ours.

> *Above all else, guard your heart, for it is the wellspring of life. Put away perversity from your mouth; keep corrupt talk far from your lips. Let your eyes look straight ahead, fix your gaze directly before you. Make level paths for your feet and take only ways that are firm.*

REFERENCES

1. Dr. Dan B. Allender, *The Healing Path: How the Hurts in Your Past Can Lead You to a More Abundant Life* (WaterBrook Press, 1999), 25.

2. "The One with the Cat," *Friends: The Complete Fourth Season* (episode 2), Writers Jill Condon and Amy Toomin, Director Shelley Jensen, (Bright/Kauffman/Crane Productions in association with Warner Bros. Television, 2003), DVD.

3. Daniel F. Case, "David and Bathsheba: Sin, Cover-up, Condemnation, and Restoration," *Case Studies*, accessed April 27, 2014, http://www.case-studies.com/david3.

4. John Phillips, *Exploring Genesis* (The Moody Bible Institute of Chicago, 1980), 99.

5. Ibid, 100.

6. John Phillips, *Bible Explorers Guide: How to Understand and Interpret the Bible* (Loizeaux Brothers, Inc. Neptune, 1987), 224.

7. Joe Namath, "Joe Namath Quotes," *BrainyQuote*, accessed April 24, 2014, http://www.brainyquote.com/quotes/authors/j/joe_namath.html#jpmUAHHWFMQ366AV.99.

8. J. Oswald Sanders, *Enjoying Intimacy with God*. Original edition ©1980 by The Moody Bible Institute of Chicago, this edition ©2000 by Discovery House Publishers. Used by permission of Discovery House Publishers, Grand Rapids, MI 49501. All rights reserved.

9. John Wesley, "Perseverance," quoted by *Sermon Illustrations*, accessed April 27, 2014, http://www.sermonillustrations.com/a-z/p/perseverance.htm.

10. "Faith: The Power to Overcome," *UCB* "The UCB Word for Today," accessed November 23, 2012, http://www.ucb.co.uk/word-for-today-13134.html. Free issues of the daily devotional are available for the UK and Republic of Ireland.

11. John Ortberg, *If You Want to Walk on Water, You've Got to Get Out of the Boat* (Zondervan, 2001), 185-186.

12. Neil Anderson, *The Bondage Breaker* (Harvest House Publishers, 2000).

13. Maier, Steven F.; Seligman, Martin E. "Learned helplessness: Theory and evidence." *Journal of Experimental Psychology*. Vol 105(1), Mar 1976, 3-46.

14. Author Unknown.

15. Marilyn Wilson and Shelly Cook Volkhardt, *Holy Habits: A Woman's Guide to Intentional Living* (NavPress, 1999), 92.

16. Used with permission.

17. John Ortberg, *If You Want to Walk on Water, You've Got to Get Out of the Boat* (Zondervan, 2001), 176, 177.

18. Ibid.

19. Carl Richardson, "Hero in the Cesspool: China's Chen Min Lin," *Beyond Borders*, accessed April 25, 2014, http://www.beyondborders.com/heroes2.html.

20. "How the Atmosphere Among a Group of Women in a Prison Camp was Transformed," Excerpt from *The Hiding Place* by Corrie Ten Boom, quoted by *Broadcaster*, accessed May 26, 2014, http://www.broadcaster.org.uk/section2/transcript/hidingplace.html.

21. Reprinted from the Preaching.com article "Four Myths about Submission in the Christian Life" by Michael Milton. Used by permission of Salem Publishing, Inc.

22. Kent Crockett, *Making Today Count for Eternity*, (Sisters, OR: Multnomah Publishers, 2001), 128, quoted by Kent Crockett, "Submission," *kentcrockett.com*, accessed May 26, 2014, http://www.kentcrockett.com/cgi-bin/illustrations/index.cgi?topic=Submission.

23. Hebrew-Greek Key Word Study Bible (KJV), Greek #5255 and #5219, (AMG Publishers), 2263, 2265.

24. Audrey Jose, *In His Image* (Lulu, 2008), 19.

www.ingramcontent.com/pod-product-compliance
Lightning Source LLC
Chambersburg PA
CBHW011343090426
42743CB00019B/3429